THE MAN WHO SKIED DOWN EVEREST

The Man Who Skied Down Everest

YUICHIRO MIURA
with ERIC PERLMAN

Published in San Francisco by HARPER & ROW, PUBLISHERS

New York / Hagerstown / San Francisco / London

Title page photograph copyright © Akira Kotani.

THE MAN WHO SKIED DOWN EVEREST Copyright © 1978 by
Yuichiro Miura and Eric Perlman. All rights reserved. Printed in the
United States of America. No part of this book may be used or
reproduced in any manner whatsoever without written permission
except in the case of brief quotations embodied in critical articles and
reviews. For information address Harper & Row, Publishers, Inc., 10
East 53rd Street, New York, N.Y. 10022. Published simultaneously in
Canada by Fitzhenry & Whiteside Limited, Toronto.

FIRST EDITION

Designed by Jim Mennick

Library of Congress Cataloging in Publication Data

Miura, Yuichiro, 1932–
   The man who skied down Everest.

   1. Miura, Yuichiro, 1932– 2. Skiers—Japan—
Biography. 3. Everest, Mount—Description.
I. Perlman, Eric, joint author. II. Title.
GV854.2.M58A35 1978   796.9'3'0924 [B] 78-3355
ISBN 0-06-250575-0

78 79 80 81 82 10 9 8 7 6 5 4 3 2 1

To my father, Keizo; my mother, Mutsu; my loving wife, Tomoko; and my children, Emily, Yuta and Gota, in special appreciation for your prayers, which brought me home safely.

And to the Sherpas who helped us, and the spirits of the eight who lost their lives.

Special thanks to Commander Charles Bowden, USNR, a good friend and lover of mountains, for editorial assistance with the original Japanese-English translation.

Contents

Prologue   1

Everest   9

First, Obstacles   21

Himalayas   37

Higher Altitudes   79

The Day Has Come   155

Miyamoto Musashi, A Brief Biographical Sketch   169

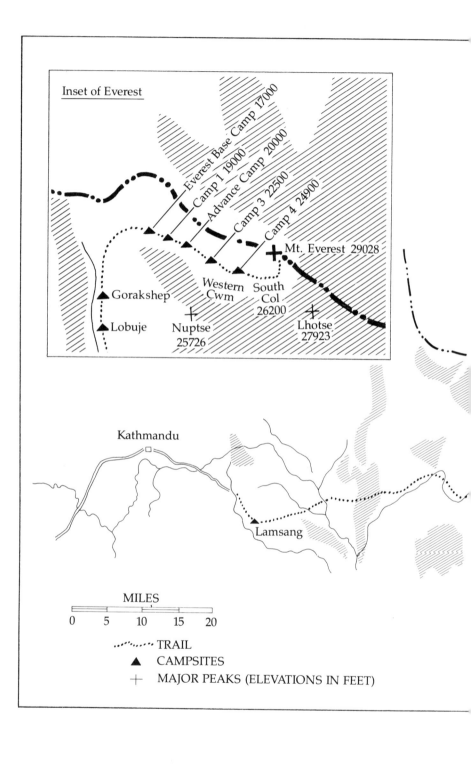

THE EVEREST AREA

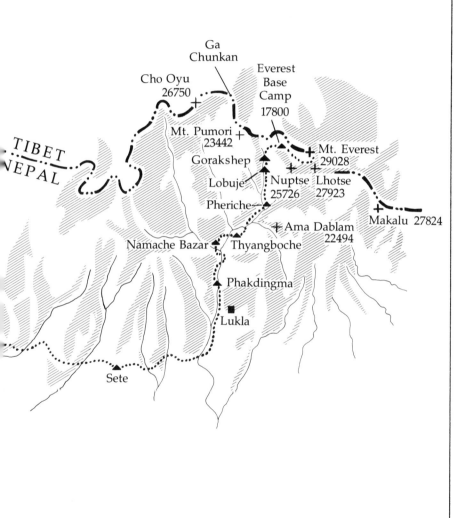

"The Way of the samurai is the resolute acceptance of death."

MIYAMOTO MUSASHI, 1645
The Way of Five Rings

Prologue

PERHAPS MINE is the story of a contemporary Icarus, the man in the ancient Greek myth who fell into the ocean and drowned, having wanted to fly in the sky. He was so overjoyed with his ingenious wax wings and a little success that he flew too close to the heavens, too close to the sun. The wax just melted away—and he died. In 1964 I achieved a speed of 107.16 miles per hour when I competed in the world speed-skiing races in Cervinia, Italy. Three times during the race I fell while schussing at speeds of more than 105 miles per hour, but I only suffered a couple of bruises on my backside, and sustained no serious injuries. Each time I got up from a fall, the Italian radio and television announcers shouted, "Miura is still alive!" It was a great surprise. Such strength! Even I was so impressed by my own resiliency of spirit and body that I thanked God and Buddha and everything in heaven and on earth.

*

I gained a strange confidence from surviving multiple falls while skiing at speeds of more than 105 miles per hour.

Speed skiing. *Photograph copyright © Keizo Miura.*

Skiing faster than 100 mph. *Photograph copyright © Keizo Miura.*

But I am not a speed maniac—I don't believe that I'm a superman or that I am in the least bit immortal. On the contrary, I get rather nervous walking in downtown Tokyo when a car speeds by or when I'm passing a building under construction. I'm always concerned that something may drop on my head or that I will fall in a hole. I'm usually a very cautious person.

But in Cervinia I told myself that to be the fastest skier in the world, I would trade my life. What I got was sixth place, and the world speed record for falling. And Japanese men earned the reputation for being very brave. I concealed my bruises and left Italy looking like a hero.

Already I was hatching a new plan.

At speed-skiing velocities, ski edges are useless for turning or stopping. Any deviation from a direct downhill trajectory instantly triggers a fall. Competition speed skiing courses all require a gradual deceleration runout with a long, flat stopping area. Few big mountains have such terrain.

If I wanted to push the limits of speed skiing to new heights and walk away alive, I had to develop a braking system. Though nobody had tried one, I thought perhaps a parachute could reduce my speed to the range of edge control. What freedom! I could ski as fast as I wanted on any mountain on earth, pop the chute, regain control, and cruise to a stop. I decided to make my first parachute attempt on Mount Fuji, the sacred mountain of my ancestors.

For many nights before the Fuji run, the greatest samurai of ancient Japan spoke to me in my dreams. The clever hero and lover Yoshitsune and the wise General Oda both urged me on. Musashi, the wandering philosopher-warrior of the seventeenth century, told me plainly: "Nobody challenges the unknown easily. You must contend with your own limitations, both real and imagined, as much as with the challenge itself."

Musashi dedicated his life completely to achieving excellence in his chosen profession—Bushido, the way of the warrior. He was a renowned philosopher, writer, and artist, as well as a champion swordsman. In his time, it was not enough to be skilled as a killer and to die well in the end; one had to embrace and employ the colors of life with equal expertise.

In my dream Musashi said: "I never regretted anything in my life. The tragedies, losses, and embarrassments were no less valuable than the joys and triumphs."

Even this fleeting contact was enough to give me a sense of historical perspective on the human quest for excellence. I realized that those who dare to do something never done before must hone their lives to no less fine an edge than did the great ones of the past. The adventurers, thinkers, and visionaries of history were giants, but greatness equal to theirs is neither more nor less attainable today than in their own time.

Only the challenges have changed. The inner tools of ingenuity, courage, and strength of will are just as difficult to wield, though rockets have replaced frigates, and computers have replaced the astrolabe and abacus.

Standing on the rim of Fuji's crown, staring at the straight and deadly run below, I experienced a momentary clarity of spirit. Everything inside me gathered to fullness. I was convinced of the possibility, but not the inevitability, of success. Other than that warm and guiding hope, my mind was utterly empty and, therefore, infinitely adjustable to the unforeseen. If it were filled with thoughts and predeterminations, it could never respond in time to necessity.

And when I launched myself into the accelerating rush of cold, white speed, I discovered a peculiarity, a pattern in my nature. Perched at the point of life and death, I like to look straight into the eye of destiny. Perhaps this is the nature of all living things: to stare with gleaming fascination down the gun barrel, as does an animal when it finds itself in the hunter's sights.

Only when I'm poised on the edge of life and death do I fully appreciate the wonder of the human experience, the

Skiing the crater of Mount Fuji. *Photograph copyright © Keizo Miura.*

beauty of humanity and the spontaneous pleasure of my inner self. Only at the threat of loss do I fully cherish what I have.

And three years later, when I plunged down the great slope of Everest, schussing the South Col headwall, I never loved life more. I struggled to evade the grasping hand of death and dispel its deepening shadows. Immersed in the world of death, my desire to live ignited.

*

Long after my success on Fuji, when I had made the decision to go to Everest and had begun the preparations, I thought of my three-year-old son, Yuta. I felt a strange sorrow, imagining his young face when he learned that he had become a child without a father. And I thought also of my newborn son, Gota. I remembered my own childhood, when I had anxiously waited for my father to come home. I recalled all the warm memories of father-and-son visits to the ocean and to the mountains, and also the times when, as a youth, my father's personality and his actions were incomprehensible, even hateful. I wondered if all other men who involved themselves in the crises of challenge thought about these painful, personal matters.

*

For the medieval samurai, to cut yourself free from your family and home was thought to be the most difficult decision, next to the final sacrifice. One of the last things an adventurer could bring himself to say was: "I have left my home. I have left everything that I love behind. Now, what is my future?" The word *adventure* sounds a little cheap to describe a commitment like this. But then, nature itself is an adventure in survival. That is the way of life.

Even when you are hard pressed on the battlefield, you should ceaselessly seek to discover the principles of strategy, and thereby develop a steady spirit.

Step by step, walk the thousand-mile road.

Study strategy and attain the spirit of the warrior. Today, gain victory over your self of yesterday; tomorrow you will triumph over greater obstacles and lesser men.

MUSASHI, *The Way of Five Rings*

1

Everest

THE EVEREST wind, usually raging, is not too bad today. It blows overhead toward the South Col, behind and above me. I have chiseled a tiny terrace on this steep wall of ice and only need to brace myself against occasional strong gusts. I have sharpened my skis to a razor's edge and polished the tips of my poles as if they were spearheads.

While climbing up the headwall to this thin and airy perch, I thought no pole could pierce the hard, icy snow. Now, I stand on the edge of finishing what I began, and the run looks skiable. But then, it has to seem skiable. I cannot turn back in shame. And despair would weaken my will and strength. In the midst of darkness, I make my own light, feeling hope where none is deserved.

What a height! I can see the yellow tent at the control center twelve thousand feet below—the size of a poppy seed. The slope is steep, averaging about forty-five degrees—a great strip of ice with no name. Looking downhill is like looking at my toes. There, at the tip of my boots, lie the distant specks of our control tent and information center. Amma, the cool and smiling second captain, and cameraman Kanau, with his imperious, hawk-like precision, are waiting for me there, watching with telescopic eyes.

According to my calculations, six seconds after take-off my speed will exceed 110 miles an hour on this eight-thousand-foot wall of ice. "Suppose the chute doesn't open?" I asked Don-chan earlier this morning in a moment of indecision. He only shook his head and smiled. "Well, I can probably find a detour, an escape route," I muttered. But that was only to console my mind. If the parachute does not open within seven seconds, I will break the world speed-skiing record—and all my bones. I picture myself falling head first down this ice wall, but quickly erase the thought.

As I stand here at the starting point, the comforting idea of a practical detour is blown away. Both sides of my route, the Geneva Spur and the once-promising south flank, are pitted with fallen stones and avalanche debris. The surface looks like sandpaper. If I ski onto either side, I will be shredded.

Months ago the expedition team had anticipated that I would feel confused at this moment. Now a precise and nagging voice comes over the headphones of the transceiver wired into my crash helmet. From the control tent down the slope at the end of the Western Cwm, Amma can see everything at a glance. He runs through the check list of preparations.

I step into my skis, adjust the oxygen flow, tighten the parachute harness, buckle my boots, and test the bindings—I am grateful for the rigid routine of thorough double checking. I forgot to strap my helmet properly. Of course, this jet pilot mask was designed with safety locks and could not fly off, but since the purpose of double protection is to keep my head intact and attached to my shoulders, I'm happy to strap it more securely.

The wind is low and the clouds are light. I think we are very lucky today. We had planned to start between eleven and twelve o'clock, but it is already past one. Usually the clouds and winds are swirling around the mountain by this time, making any skiing impossible. But this day, as if it were waiting for us to finish our task, the sea of clouds lies nowhere near Mount Everest, although a few tufts cling near the summit. The high and distant peaks of Pumori, Cho Oyu, and Gachunkan hold the clouds under control.

I have trained myself to set up all my equipment systems with gloves on, but today I want to be certain everything is absolutely right, and use my bare hands. Within half an hour my knuckles are like wood, and I have lost all feeling in my fingertips—a mild case of frostbite.

Otaki's Bell & Howell movie camera has been tested to ten degrees below zero. Today it became inoperable, and he has had to warm the metal and plastic next to his stomach. Even in bright sunlight and light winds, Mount Everest is brutally cold.

*

I Don't Feel Any Fear

I'd better get busy. Amma reports that the wind is from the south, coming upslope at twelve miles an hour at Camp 4. The voice over the CB in my helmet is loud and clear. The wind is blowing right into the great bosom of Mount Everest, then bouncing back, whirling sideways and down. Though the weather and wind predictions are useful, I must make my own judgments in these last moments.

I have decided to move the take-off point about thirty-five yards closer to the Geneva Spur to the north so that I can ski a cleaner and more direct line, heading more toward the south wall. I wonder what the lower slope is really like—the snow conditions, surface features, and obstacles. That is the key question, but it is already too late to find out.

No mountaineer has ever tried to climb up this slope before—this dangerous wall of ice—and I am trying to ski down it with only the information obtained by peering through a telescope. Seen with the naked eye from a distance, you would probably say, "Oh, what a steep hill, what a dramatic slope!" Up close, it is a beautiful, hard wall of ice. Just studying it with a telescope you can see how wild it looks, plunging from the mouth of the Geneva Spur. Gusts of snow swirl in blinding whirlwinds across the face. Rocks poke out of the ice. Overhead, clouds boil and charge in changing winds.

Nothing looks very encouraging, but, to be honest, there is no fear in my mind, no shaking in my body. There is no trace of that dreadful feeling I know so well, that of being chased by something unknown, with nowhere to escape to, like a desperate animal with no refuge. I have stood at the starting gates of too many races, at the lips of too many deadly runs, fighting that awful feeling. Great ski racers break free from terror with an explosion of energy and determination. There is no need for that today.

No reflective voice is asking, "What will happen to me now?" I have become empty, pure perception. I'm not being philosophical. I think I have even forgotten that I am supposed to go down a mountain on skis. I am not nervous; there is nothing.

*

Take-Off

A great wind, a wind of my own making, equal to my speed—it grows as I accelerate and forms an ever-hardening wall. In a moment the parachute will open.

Just as I expected, the wall of ice beneath my feet is wild and deadly—twisted, rippled, torn, and strewn with embedded fallen rocks. My ski edges, sharpened like twin samurai swords, and the spearhead of my poles are completely useless on this hard ice. I cannot stop, braking is hopeless. I pop the parachute.

The jet stream is invisible as it blows from the mountain peak to the south wall, then tumbles down the

Take off!! *Photograph copyright © Kazunari Yasuhisa.*

rocky sides of the Geneva Spur. Its power has blown down and deformed my chute. I am jerked and swung like a string puppet in the hands of a thoughtless child.

Desperate, my mind shouts and chatters: "This useless parachute! Get out, escape—to the Lhotse climbing route, or ski down into the third camp area, the icy terrace—find an escape route!"

As I hurtle between the rocks of the Geneva Spur, I am suddenly spewn across a swath of lumpy, glassy ice. All the escape routes I had considered are hopeless. I am utterly out of control, a runaway rockfall of one.

Suddenly, I am pulled up short. Contorted and crushed by my own speed and torque, I don't even realize that the inevitable has happened. I have fallen. The meter in my head starts ticking: 99, then 99.99, showing the tiny percent left of my life, moving toward death.

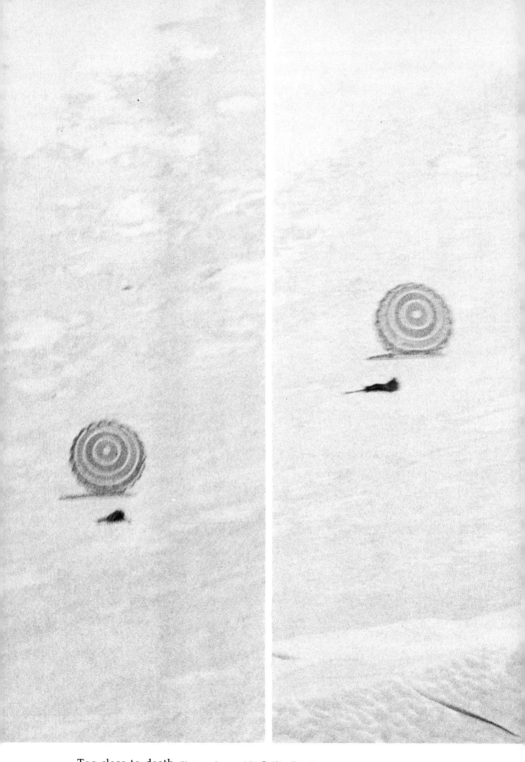

Too close to death. *Photographs copyright © Akira Kotani.*

Time is slowing. I feel the ice wall on my back and fall, fall, falling. The skis have ripped from my feet. There is no way to stop. The surface of this ice is so hard that even an ice ax doesn't chip it. My fingernails would do no good. Just ten seconds more—in about ten seconds I shall be thrown off the tip of the glacier into the dark blue void of ice.

I wonder what it feels like at the moment of death. I am only mildly curious and slightly interested now. My experience of myself balloons into a slow and vacuous ballet. I am saying good-by to my life. I am saying good-by to being a human.

I wonder what happens at the moment of cutting away, but even more, I feel a tremendous emptiness. Was life nothing but a dream? The word keeps rolling in my head. I wonder if this is the instinct of all living things—to disbelieve life when faced with its end.

Idly, I wonder if the parachute is still open at all, and I look up. The parachute looks like a loyal animal, a creature from another world. It is swaying from left to right, big, round, red, and useless. In a desperate effort to gain control, I pull at the cord with my right hand. Then I realize that the rock—the very one about which I had decided long before I started, "It will be the end if I ever hit that rock"—is looming closer and closer. It looks like a house, doors flung open, bearing down. There is no escape. Time has stopped—now.

*

I am alive and conscious, lying with my face on my arms, sprawled across a steep stretch of rock-encrusted ice. The Bergschrund, the gigantic, yawning crevasse, lies only a few yards down the slope.

I have to shake my head, bumping the helmet two or three times on the ice, just to make sure that I am truly a human being again. I feel so sentimental and nostalgic about being myself, and not dead. I'm giddy with joy, but this is still a wall of ice I'm on, and there's very little distance between me and the waiting Bergschrund. I try to chisel away a little ice with my ski boots. I am lying on top of a two-inch dusting of powder snow. Underneath lies cold ice, looking at me with shark's eyes. I start to slide, little by little. The receiver in my helmet starts to scream, "Don't move, Yuichiro, please don't move!" Is that Amma's familiar, precise voice? Then I see three friends and two Sherpas picking their way across the ice field. I am alive and safe! *But what does that mean? And what does it matter that I continue to struggle in this world and not some other?*

Since the magnetic darkness of death has drawn back—for a while—the bright play of living reclaims my best efforts.

There is timing in everything. Timing in strategy cannot be mastered without considerable practice.

Timing is essential in dancing and music; without it there is neither harmony nor rhythm. Timing and rhythm are just as important in the military arts—shooting bows and guns, and riding horses. Timing is the essence of all skills and abilities.

There is even timing in the Void.

Timing dominates the whole life of the warrior, in his thriving and declining, in his harmony and discord. It is the same for the merchant in the rise and fall of capital.

All things entail rising and falling; you must be able to discern and utilize the patterns of timing amid life's changes.

In strategy there is a spectrum of timing factors. From the beginning you must perceive applicable and inapplicable timings; you must pick the relevant timing from the milieu of events: distance and background, fast and slow, large and small. Background timing is the key to good strategy—you must integrate your position with the overall pattern of changes, otherwise your strategy will become uncertain.

Win your battles by acting from the timing of the Void, tempered with the timing of intelligence which perceives the enemies' patterns. Thus, respond with superior timing and catch the enemy unawares.

MUSASHI "Ring of Earth"

2

First, Obstacles

I SAT in Kenji Fukuhara's tidy living room in the Roppongi district of Tokyo. I had just come back from skiing in New Zealand. Kenji told me to be sure to come visit him because the chief officer of the Nepalese government's travel bureau was in Tokyo to screen a travelogue that Kenji and his team had filmed in Nepal. Since I was thinking that I would love to ski in the Himalayas, I went to visit him immediately.

The small, gentlemanly chief of the travel bureau shook hands with me in Nepalese style, and we all sat down and looked at the rushes. Every time an image of snowy mountains flashed on the screen, I asked myself, "Could I ski that slope, could I ski this mountain?" My appetite was whetted. That evening, Kenji and I discussed skiing in the Himalayas. A Japanese Alpine Club member, Teru Takahashi, suggested Mount Dhaulagiri. Pictures of the mountain looked vicious. He said I could probably ski somewhere on it, though I really wasn't too interested. But, if it was supposed to be the best skiing in·the Himalayas, I thought I would look into it. I could tell already what the others were thinking—if you are going to ski in the Himalayas at all, Mount Everest is the one. The idea was almost taboo, however. Everyone felt it was absolutely impossible. As if reading their minds, the chief of the Nepalese travel bureau said: "How about Everest? International climbing regulations and reservation schedules will be all drawn up by next February, so come to Katmandu then."

*

Everyone got right to work. The effort involved would have been enough to help some underdeveloped nation become independent. We had no capital, equipment or offices, but we decided to push ahead anyway.

The budget—some people said it would take $25,000 and some said $1 million. Most said it was impossible, no matter how much money it took. We agreed a minimum of $300,000 was necessary.

My friend Matsushita, an advertising executive, talked Tokyo University into giving us a small, oddly shaped room on the seventh floor of the science and technology building. I think it used to be a storage room. We made it the headquarters of the Everest tactical planning squad. It soon became the Miura Ski Research Room.

Day after day the room throbbed with excited talk and detailed planning. There, cloistered in the concrete bowels of academia, our dreams carried us to the open sky and snow fields of the Himalayas.

*

Fantasies and Protocol

We had to have official-sounding titles to convince sponsors to give us the necessary funds. We gave Matsushita the title of business manager, and Teru Takahashi the title of expedition leader because he knew the Nepalese government; I took the title of representative—vague and noncommittal, but enough to start the action.

Soon, things began to happen. A team of professional mountaineers gathered around us. We knew, in any case, that we needed permission from the government of Nepal to climb the mountain. And we knew that for the last five years the Nepalese government had been having territorial disputes with the Chinese government and had not been issuing any permits to climb the mountains near the border. No matter how much money or talent we collected, we would not be able to move without official permission.

As expedition captain, Takahashi was growing very excited. He was continually scheming, "Well, if you talk to so and so, or if you do such and such and so forth . . ." Listening to his mumbling was like listening to an enemy spy, but it all sounded very promising.

Takahashi mentioned a professional mountaineer nicknamed Don-chan. He was Japan's top rock and ice climbing specialist, a world-class mountaineer with impeccable leadership qualities. He was forceful and friendly, and he possessed a passionate drive for success.

"But I have just come back from South America," said Don-chan, wiping his forehead, when he finally came to our headquarters in the science building. He had climbed in the Himalayas for five seasons, and he was the first man to ascend Gachunkan. He was one of the most honored mountaineers in Japan. Besides, he was a section chief in an import–export company and spoke fluent English, the international climbers' language. Amid much laughter, we persuaded him to join our expedition.

Takahashi and Don-chan flew to Nepal to negotiate for the Everest expedition papers in January.

*

Permission Granted

When we met them at the Tokyo airport, they looked like the heroic survivors of some international spy war who had just succeeded in snatching the secret documents. Don-chan joked as he kept looking around to see if there were enemy agents still on his tail. We talked late into the night about the bureaucratic wringer they had been through. The official papers from the Nepalese government gave the Japan-Everest ski expedition permission to ski down from the South Col of Mount Everest. There were two time periods allowed: one in the fall of the 1969 post-monsoon season for scouting, and one in 1970 during the spring pre-monsoon season. In return, we had to give a copy of our documentary film to the Nepalese government. We were elated. Of the ten applications from all over the world for permission to climb Everest, Japan had applied for it last and been the first to succeed.

*

When I talked to professional mountaineers, my plans sounded like a complete joke. I told many people that this was going to be a computer adventure. I am embarrassed every time I think about what I said back then. The plan was that I would install some sort of electronic, remote control system in the skis which would control their direction and angle of edging according to my speed and trajectory, the wind velocity, and the surface condition of the slope. I was completely taken by my imaginative machinations, which even a child with a little scientific knowledge would judge impossible.

I was a little boy looking for a new weapon to conquer the world. Our practical team of mountaineers tried to cool off this crazy skier, but it was like arguing with Don Quixote. They spoke in detail about the grave dangers of climbing in the Himalayas: rockfalls, avalanches, 120-mile-an-hour winds, and vicious storms. "Even if you are very tough, once you get past sixteen thousand feet, you can die of altitude sickness just like that, Yu-chan," they said to me. Thin air and lack of oxygen are just as deadly as a storm. Also, it is very difficult for a person who has never been there to judge personal, psychological compatibility with the Himalayas. The awesome power and desolation of those mountains are enough to overwhelm the mind and drive you mad.

For these practical-minded mountain climbers, my plans to ski down a mountain that had given the world's foremost mountaineers so much trouble so far—it was like dealing with a maniac. I wonder how they ever thought of hauling me and all my wild machinery up the side of Mount Everest, a mountain with so many obstacles. Still, ignoring their misgivings, the mountaineers went ahead with their preparations: the schedules, the equipment, food, porters, Sherpas—a thousand details, every one important.

*

I talked about airplanes, helicopters, rockets, and then I remembered seeing an ad in a newspaper about a dirigible flying over Tokyo with flashing color advertisements on its side, and I thought, "Wouldn't that be great—flying slowly over the Himalayas to Mount Everest, and then landing on the South Col." A few days later the man who imported the dirigible to Japan came to visit our headquarters. Even the doubting mountaineers began to realize that this fantasy was becoming a reality when the owner said, "Yes, why not, it sounds rather interesting to fly over Katmandu with a dirigible," and offered it for our use.

*

This is the Way of conduct for those who want to master strategy:

1. Think truly, with no dishonesty or deceit.
2. The Way lies in training.
3. Become acquainted with every art and science.
4. Know the Ways of all professions.
5. Distinguish between gain and loss in worldly matters.
6. Develop intuitive understanding and accurate judgment for everything.
7. See the unseen, know the unknown.
8. Pay attention even to trifles.
9. Do nothing which is useless.

MUSASHI "Ring of Earth"

*

Body Power

If I was going to ski down Mount Everest, I had to do it my own way: faster than sixty miles an hour and equipped with a control parachute. In that altitude and terrain I also needed an oxygen tank, safety jacket, mask and helmet with a transceiving system installed inside. I was already thirty-five, and when the actual time came, I would be thirty-seven. I understood my body; I was no longer as vigorous as I had been at twenty or at thirty. Then, I could do just about anything and not be bothered. Now, I was beginning to feel my age, but it was too late to think about it; I had to prepare myself for the challenge of my life.

*

Midnight was the training time for the ancient samurai. Free from prying, inquisitive eyes, he honed his skills in the shadowy forest. Sword in hand, he raced through the trees, nipping off leaves as he passed.

Though our expedition offices were in Tokyo, I lived in Kamakura, a town on the sea many miles away. Weary from endless planning and talk every night, I would return on the midnight train to the station three miles from home. Only then could I shake free of the worrisome papers and meetings of the day and run the miles of beach toward home.

Eight hundred years before, on this same beach, my family fought against the warlord Taira clan. We lost the bitter and bloody battle and fled from our homeland to the mountainous north. The Taira clan was extinguished in later wars, and Miura blood had now returned to enjoy this seashore and prepare for battles to come.

With the rich sound of the sea running in my ears, I imagined the sand was steep snow. The stars were snowflakes, and the sea foam was drifted powder. I swooped and carved turns as I ran through the night. Triumphant, I trained for a war only I could lose.

*

I decided to pay attention to my eating habits. In the spring of 1967, while starring in a ski film, I landed poorly on a jump and sprained my Achilles tendon. I was hospitalized. Three months later, I went to ski on Mount Popocatepetl in Mexico and ate too much Mexican food. By the time I got back to Japan I was so fat I couldn't even walk fast. I gasped every time I tried to run.

With the Everest mission approaching, I began to worry. Many times I felt I should give up this crazy plan altogether. I pictured how my body would react to the cold, the freezing winds and the extreme altitudes of the Himalayas. I started studying books on nutrition and health.

Unfortunately, all those were just normal diet books written for average people trying to live healthy everyday lives, free from sickness. There was nothing designed to create a superman for the Himalayas. I searched for help everywhere.

*

Simian Nutrition

I had studied veterinary science in college, done research in pharmaceutical science, passed the Japanese national licensing exam, and worked as a neurophysiology researcher at Hokkaido University's veterinary science study room. Of course, I had forgotten most of it, but I still knew something about biology and nutrition.

I began to read offbeat books on nutrition and ran across ideas and theories that completely contradicted what I used to believe. For instance, I read that "the Japanese digestive system was not made to process large quantities of meat." I began to feel embarrassed that I gobbled meat like a wolf, assuming that flesh would give me muscle. As I thought about it, I realized that Sherpas, people who were incredibly strong at high altitudes, hardly ate any meal at all. They were grain-eating people. I imagined their eating habits, trying to recall the stories I had heard from people who had been to the Himalayas.

One day I came across an enlightening hint. It went something like this: "Humans are primates who have evolved parallel to other primates, like monkeys and gorillas. These latter hardly eat any meat at all, and their usual diet consists of fruit, bananas, nuts, sprouts of grasses and buds of trees; look at the energy of the gorilla and the chimpanzee, the agility of their actions, their supple strength. Human beings began to eat meat, and now look at them, diseased and overweight. Lions and tigers eat meat. Though they look very powerful, observe them closely. They spend most of their lives napping." When I read this, being naive, I was impressed.

For someone like me, who loves fruit, raw food was an easy diet to follow. Since it was summer, I asked my wife to pile our dining table with watermelons, grapes and all kinds of fruits. I refused meat, of course, and even ignored the rice, eating just what was on the dining table. When I went out, I pretended to be a Hindu vegetarian and ate only salad and fruit.

As for training, I was so fat in the beginning that I weighed 160 pounds. I had to give up running because my feet hurt, my tendons ached, and I ran out of breath. That's the embarrassing truth. I took to riding a bicycle, crawling up the street like a snail on my flashy racer.

Imagine a professional skier thinking about skiing down Mount Everest, too fat to run and eating only fruit so that he'd become like a chimpanzee. It would have seemed funnier if my life weren't on the line. I continued my training program for about a month.

Truly, it happened. I started to lose weight. I became lighter, and I was able to run and ride my bicycle, fast. I regained my endurance and breath control. My weight went down to 150 pounds; I had lost 10 pounds in two weeks, with no decrease in energy. I was so proud that I began to tell everyone about my raw food program. One day on the way to Tokyo from Osaka on the "bullet" train, I ran into some men from a Japanese bodybuilding society. Of course I had to brag about my theory of gorillas and chimpanzees. One of them opened his eyes wide with revelation: "Of course, gorillas and chimpanzees only eat fruit, and look at their physiques!" We ate tangerines the rest of the trip.

As summer ended, the weather turned cold. I don't

know what happened, but the more I ate tangerines and persimmons, the colder I felt. The little fall breezes felt like the night winds of winter. It had never seemed so cold before at this time of the year. When other people were in shirt-sleeves, I was already chilled and reaching for a sweater. Usually, I hate hot weather and have proudly taken the cold very well, but not that year.

Then I remembered that animals of tropical zones eat fruit to cool their body temperature, and animals in cold places eat nuts, grains, and roots to keep warm. Aha! Gorillas and chimpanzees are from the tropics, and the Himalayas are cold. I remembered scenes from documentary films and stories of climbing expeditions in the Himalayas; at least one or two members of every team had been frostbitten severely and lost some fingers or toes. I began to be concerned that with my current heat-generating capacity my entire body might be frostbitten. Besides, how was I ever going to transport to the Himalayas the mountains of fruit I would need?

My raw fruit diet didn't work in the cold, so I decided to improve it. I came up with a recipe that I called my "superhuman diet."

Slimy foods are good for building up energy; so for breakfast I grated a raw potato into a mixing bowl, added a couple of raw eggs, and splashed in a little natural vinegar. I left the concoction to ferment and grow moldy. Then I just whipped it up with a little soy sauce, let it get foamy, and drank it. Sometimes I added sticky beans and seaweed.

I don't know how my wife ever put up with her insane husband's eating habits. Fortunately, my children were able to escape my fruit diet. But they were influenced by my superhuman menu that followed, and began to avoid chemicals and preservatives. Instead, they would eat what their father ate—things like small fish all the way down to the bone, and piles of fresh vegetables. They became very healthy and lithe and caught few colds.

*

Money?

My physical training seemed to be going all right, but the funding wasn't getting anywhere. The expedition master plan had become a wild fantasy.

Everybody on the team believed that the skier could get the money. "Why don't we let the skier worry about fund raising, and we'll just think about climbing," they said. I thought this myself and said, "Of course there will be money for this great project. It's the adventure of the century." I also believed that this was such a great opportunity for a Japanese person to triumph that the government would give me some support.

All this talk and fantasizing led nowhere. We were falling into a deeper financial hole every day, and finally had reached the point where we wondered how we were going to get money for lunch. When we had started, we had each chipped in several thousand dollars, but that was all gone.

*

By the fall of 1969 we would need ten or twenty thousand dollars for the Everest scouting trip. Furthermore, I had promised to do a South American ski trip for a major Japanese newspaper and found that I didn't even have enough money for that. Straining my mind to find a solution to my problem, I suddenly remembered that in the very beginning, when we had received a cable from Katmandu saying we had gotten permission from the government of Nepal to try the downhill on Mount Everest, I had received a telephone call in the early morning from someone who spoke Japanese with a heavy accent asking me, "Are you intending to do this expedition under the Japanese flag or somebody else's flag?" He said he was a foreign correspondent from another country. As a rather patriotic person, I gave him a very vague answer; I hoped to do it for the Japanese people especially. I would have liked to be able to say in the end that we, the Japanese people, with all our spirit and skill, together had accomplished this dream. We really did not want any other country's support or foreign funds from some cola company to sponsor the trip. But what could we do? I began to think that perhaps we could sell our bodies but keep our souls.

*

Mr. Akai

If we were going to have foreign support, why not the biggest? How about the U.S. Department of State? I contacted Mr. Akai, the electronics magnate. I remembered that when I skied with him years before, he was accompanying an important figure from the U.S. State Department. I called Akai-san very casually, and he responded just like any neighborhood man—very friendly and personable. He was willing to see me and listen to my ideas. I met him in the president's room of his company's elegant office building near Tokyo International Airport.

*

Matsushita, the business manager of the expedition, and I were worn out. We had no money or equipment. All we had were endless words and ideas. Of course we had tried our best; we didn't just run around wasting our energy. We had drawn up a rather sensible budget and a clear proposal defining our purposes and personal obligations for the project. We had stated that this expedition was to expand the possibilities of mankind by joining the hands of humanity and science. It sounded a little grandiose, but it was very impressive, and most importantly, we believed it ourselves.

After listening to our plan very carefully, Mr. Akai offered us some tea. He said, "Well, I know some people—I have some connection with the U.S. State Department—but truly, how much do you really need to realize this plan?" By this time, we had summed up our budget estimates and everybody had agreed on $420,000 as the total cost. Most people, when they heard this figure, politely switched the subject, but Mr. Akai—his voice sounded to me like some beneficent god from heaven—said, "If it's possible, I would like to offer you the whole amount." I could only gulp!

*

A Game Becomes an Expedition

I think this was the first time the expedition sounded feasible. We had believed that the plan was possible, but there had been nothing concrete. We had all said that we could borrow some money, but we had already spent what we had, and we knew no bank would sponsor this crazy idea.

Before any expedition gets started, there's always a cold wind of doubt that threatens its survival. It takes a great deal of effort to sail in this wind, to surmount the crushing waves of a critical world. Especially when trying to do something big, you've got to have timing—good luck in meeting and convincing people. If Mr. Saburo Akai had not appeared, I doubt we could have even left Japan.

*

Getting It Together

Finally, what had been called an expedition game began to come together both in spirit and in reality. In the middle of July 1969, I headed for South America for a month's ski training with Akira Kotani, the dour, bearded philosopher who was to be head photographer on the Everest expedition. Our training program was ambitious. We planned to test our endurance at the tip of South America's great mountain spine, against blizzards and treacherous cold, and, if possible, try downhill skiing on the highest mountain of South America, Aconcagua, 22,831 feet above sea level. For the last year and a half, I and everybody around me had been running around getting nowhere, just mouthing, "Everest, Everest." At least now we could see a speck of light. We all had to begin basic physical training immediately. Though my heart was really in the preparation for the Everest expedition, I felt that this training trip would also rejuvenate my spirit as well as my body.

*

The ski trip in South America was wonderful, and on arrival back at the expedition office in Tokyo I was ready to dedicate myself totally to preparing for the Everest expedition. When I walked in the door, Matsushita and Takahashi did not look too happy to see me. Once again we had run out of money. Even with the help of Mr. Akai, the more money that came in, the more went out. Matsushita called me aside and said, "If everything falls apart and it doesn't come off, I will lower my head and apologize, so that's all right, don't worry." First, I was flabbergasted, and then I grew angry. People were talking about giving up, when we hadn't even left Japan. Even Takahashi, usually with a smile on his face, looked glum and beaten. I don't really blame them; I guess it was my fault, thinking everything was under control and traipsing off to South America. *Success and depression are equally dangerous. Both tend to make you lose sight of the continuous, changing flow of events.*

*

The Chinese philosopher Mencius said, "Whenever heaven is about to bestow a great office on anyone, it first tempers his mind with suffering, and his sinews and bones with toil; it toughens his body with hunger and subjects him to poverty and failure. In all these ways it awakens his spirit, strengthens his weaknesses and fulfills his character."

"Well," I thought, "if we are out of ideas, if we are out of money, let's get some more." The only way was to attract new people with new ideas. But Matsushita and Takahashi were not convinced. They had put so much credence into their doubts and despair that they never regained their confidence. Eventually, they quit the project.

Looking around for new ideas, I met the great Japanese writer, Taisuke Fujishima. He was a school friend of Kotani, the cameraman. "Well," he said, "if you are having trouble, why don't you go see Mr. Ishihara, the movie producer? He has great courage, and he will probably help you." Taisuke was absolutely right. Ishihara loved the idea of someone skiing Mount Everest and decided to produce a professional documentary film on it. The famous producer Isao Zeniya took charge of making the movie and began to work with us full time. Up to this point, the Yomiuri Newspaper Company, largest in Japan, had been uncertain about their interest, but now they decided to send three reporters from their main office. The Everest adventure was back on its feet and running.

The spirit of my school of strategy is based on water. Words cannot explain the Way in detail, but they can guide you toward an intuitive grasp. Read a word, then think about it. If you interpret the meaning as only applicable to battle, you will mistake the Way.

The principles of strategy are conveyed in terms of single combat, but you must think broadly; the principles are equally applicable for ten-thousand-a-side battles and the lonely, internal struggle for wisdom.

If you merely read, you can not know the Way of strategy. Absorb the principles of strategy in your heart and express them in action.

In strategy your spiritual bearing is no different than normal. Both in fighting and everyday life you should be determined but calm. Meet the situation with your spirit poised and unbiased, neither tense nor recklessly fierce. Even when your body is relaxed, do not let your spirit go limp. An elevated spirit is weak and a low spirit is weak. Do not let the enemy see your spirit.

Small people must understand the spirit of large people, and large people must understand the spirit of small people. Whatever your size, do not be misled by the reactive fears and uncertainties of your own body.

With your spirit open and free, look at all things with a broad and high perspective. Polish your wisdom, learn compassion and justice, distinguish between good and evil, study the Ways of different arts. When you cannot be deceived by any man or any situation, you will have realized the wisdom of strategy.

MUSASHI "Ring of Water"

3

Himalayas

IN SEPTEMBER of 1969 some of the Everest team members and I went to Nepal for advance scouting and skiing. The luggage was shipped, and the team left under the leadership of Don-chan. Before I knew it, I was flying out of Tokyo airport, feeling as if I'd left important equipment and bits of myself behind. I reached Katmandu and found myself checked into a room in the Hotel Shankar, a very old and ornate hotel, like a king's palace.

I felt tired, as if my body had lain unused for ages and was encrusted with rust. I wondered if I could really climb Mount Everest. For a tryout, I jogged around the town of Katmandu.

I felt as if I had slipped through a time warp. Everybody who arrives in this town has the same reaction—stepping out of a jet airplane, you feel as if you are suddenly thrown into a medieval market place. Enveloped by tumultuous gaiety and confusion, you are lost in a strange world of barter and trade. Once you step into this town you are drawn into a Lilliputian maze, and you feel you will never be able to get out. It's a kind of magical feeling. Time stops in this place, and, floating in the unfamiliar scents and colors, I almost forgot what I came here for.

I really wanted to jog, but my legs seemed heavy and stiff. After running only half a mile, my muscles were aching and tight, and I was completely out of breath. "How can I get up Everest? I might even collapse before I get there." *Body, you must grow strong.*

*

I waited for our preliminary scouting expedition to begin, overshadowed by a strange pessimism. In the front lawn of the hotel I did about ten push-ups and tried to stand on my head. My arms were like rubber, and I said to myself: "I'm as limp as a *soba* noodle. I can't climb anything." I was supposed to train my body, sharpen my mind, and work on ski technique. I was supposed to build myself up as a man fit for the heroic job of skiing down Everest. I came all the way here with Mount Everest dancing in front of my eyes. And here was this disgusting, degenerate body. My pulse was above seventy, even in the early morning, still in bed. "Why is my pulse so high? Why am I so tired even before I start?"

*

The camera crew caravan had left for Base Camp at the foot of Everest two weeks earlier. The leader was Tomio Saeki—or "Tonko," as we called him—the champion drinker of the Japanese Alps. A vigorous, happy rebel, he hated bureaucracy and loved to let events take their own course. With his perennial good humor and natural camaraderie with the Sherpas and porters, he was the perfect commander for this scouting caravan of 250 porters and tons of equipment on its way through the steady, drenching downpour of high monsoon season.

Assisting Tonko on this unremarkable human pack train was "Genius" Yassan, the ice-eyed rock climber. Strong, silent and totally controlled, Yassan was like a *ninja*, a professional assassin. His strength and clear-headedness were a great asset to the team. It was a blow to us all when, long after the Everest expedition, we heard he had been buried in an avalanche on Manaslu, another Himalayan peak.

Genius's best friend, Ishiguro, went on the caravan too. Eldest son of one of the richest families in Japan, Ishiguro looked like a big, dumb, muscle man. Actually, he was an extremely intelligent and sensitive professional architect.

Dr. Yamada, the good-natured sawbones, completed the four-man team in charge of taking equipment up to Everest Base Camp. Screaming their heads off in this insane rainfall, they had left for twenty-five days of a long, long trek.

*

The second team, which included myself, Don-chan and seven others, flew into Everest Base Camp about two weeks later. On a beautiful bright morning, nine of us got into two aircraft, a twin-engine Otter and the United Nations-chartered Swiss mountain airplane, and we flew over a two-week caravan route in little more than an hour.

Lukla, Everest's airport, was built by the first conqueror of Mount Everest, Sir Edmund Hillary. From there, it would take less than a week to reach Base Camp, located at the foot of the Khumbu icefall.

In Tibetan, Lukla means "place with many goats and sheep." The airfield consists of a little terrace of grass on a steep hill, perched among some deadly looking canyons. Trying to land on this strip is an acrobatic gamble, and the Japanese Alpine Club's chartered Nepalese Air Force plane ran right into the ground. The wing ripped off and was still lying at the edge of the runway.

*

In the language of the Sherpas, bala means "large" or "big." Bala sabu means "leader." I was bala sabu of the ski team. For the writer Taisuke Fujishima, we added an extra *bala* to his name because he was commander-in-chief. But his friends were more concerned about when he would be *bala bala,* which means, in Japanese, "falling apart."

Last year, when Taisuke went to Nepal to discuss plans for the Nepalese pavilion for the Osaka World Fair, he had some spare time, so he took a trip to Lukla. He managed to talk his way on board another one of the Nepal Air Force planes. That one, too, had an accident. The airplane fell apart during the landing. The Nepalese Air Force was left with only one airplane, and didn't feel like carrying any more Japanese passengers. Taisuke had to return on a United Nations plane.

*

This scouting expedition was probably the weakest Himalayan climbing team ever. I knew nothing about the mountain. I was the leader of the whole thing, with the title of captain. Actually, I was more like a guest of honor. Don-chan had really organized everything. The team included two skiers, some people from the movies and newspapers, and a slew of photographers—all these people were excess baggage; the only professional mountain climbers were Don-chan, Yassan, and Ishiguro.

When we finally reached Everest Base Camp, I tried out my skis on the harsh Himalayan snow. For some reason, my endurance against the high mountains was not as bad as I had expected. I was able to test my parachute on an icy face twenty thousand feet above sea level. That day we had forgotten to bring our lunches. Everybody yammered as if they were starving to death, saying "Let's go home"—it was no better than a kindergarten excursion!

*

Up and Down

I discovered the pleasure of talking to myself during our first expedition in the Himalayas. In today's busy world, in modern life, people always try to explain themselves to each other. They try so hard to convince others, but they rarely talk to themselves. As I walk along in the green breeze or in the sun, or at the edge of a creek, or in the field, in the forest, or on the glacier alone, I find a great person to listen to my conversation—myself. I look in my heart and continue the conversation with no lies or excess criticism of faults.

As I strolled around the foot of Mount Everest, I wondered, "What will you think about at the height of twenty-five thousand feet? What will you regret?" "I will probably regret coming all the way here," I replied to myself.

The Nepalese liaison officer who accompanied us on our scouting trip got his first taste of high altitude life at our Base Camp, seventeen thousand feet above sea level. He said, "In Nepal we should abandon our prisons; if anybody does something wrong, we should just send them up into our high mountains."

I suppose it is necessary for those of us who don't do good deeds all our lives to come to this height for purification. Professional mountaineers become so aware of themselves, so strongly introspective, perhaps in response to the pain and stress of high elevations. That's why, consciously or unconsciously, they repeat the examples of monks and ascetics and pick places like this to be with themselves.

*

One of the religious Sherpas, before he joined us on this strange expedition, decided to go to Mount Khumbila, the sacred mountain which towers above an isolated Sherpa village. The Sherpa went to talk to a hermit who had lived on the mountain longer than anybody could remember. The hermit said, "Sherpa, you people from the east, there will be a bad star on the eastern sky, so you must be cautious."

Sherpa means "people from the east," and come to think of it, we Japanese are also from the east. The message was foreboding.

Unfortunately, the hermit's words were prophetic. The Sherpa Phu Dorje, a great mountaineer and stalwart friend, did not come back from Mount Everest. He was scouting the Khumbu icefall when the ground gave way. With a roaring crack, a crevasse opened up, and great blocks of ice bounded down the hill. Phu Dorje disappeared, and we never recovered his body.

His laugh was like sunshine, his spirit was bright and strong. He was a hero of Nepal, and now he was gone, swallowed in the unmarked, blue-white grave of the icefall of Khumbu.

Our scouting trip ended and we returned to Tokyo. We were confident of success, but we knew we could never taste true triumph, now that death had struck our team. We suffered an untenable loss before we'd really begun.

*

Back in Katmandu

We had another six months of preparation in Tokyo, and then the expedition began in earnest. Our organizational nightmare somehow made its way through the dark, and we found ourselves back in Katmandu in February 1969 in pre-monsoon season.

We had decided that the bare, icy, snow fields of spring were preferable to the avalanching powder so prevalent in the post-monsoon season, which started in late September.

We checked into the Hotel Shankar again, and this time I started my sun-bathing right away on the hotel's front lawn. I remembered the consternation I caused last year among the modest Sherpa families.

We had camped at Namche Bazar, the Sherpa capital, which consisted of about fifty small houses in the tiny village square. The village was surrounded by a soaring wall of Himalayas. We could see Everest from the top of a nearby hill. The hilltop was a great spot, blessed with good weather. The local yaks—Tibetan cows—walked around gracefully, as if they were in butter and cheese commercials. I was feeling so great that I decided to get a sun tan. I took off my clothes down to my briefs, put on some sun-tan lotion, and took a nap.

One of the head Sherpas, Ang Tsering, got very upset. Apparently, if any Sherpa lies down naked, he is proposing to the girl of his choice. My behavior caused quite a commotion among the perpetual bevy of surrounding children and young girls. They acted as if they were seeing a rare animal at the zoo.

Besides making the mistake of proposing in broad daylight, I caught cold from showing off. Everybody told me I would get sick, but I haughtily replied that I had trained myself in the ocean and enjoyed the chill. The result was quite dreadful. At night I had a high fever, and for the next four days I could barely keep up with the rest of the caravan.

This time, I was determined to get in top shape. I jogged to a Hindu "Monkey Temple," built about two thousand years ago at the foot of a hill dense with jungle vegetation. I almost collapsed running up the long flight of stone steps. The thunderclap from the deafening gong, combined with the shouted prayers of the Hindu monks and the heavy pall of incense, made me nearly pass out, and I narrowly escaped falling by clinging to one of the temple columns. On the way back down, I tripped and slammed my foot on the cobblestone stairs. As a result I could barely walk up the hotel steps. I thought for sure that I had broken my toe, but the doctor said it was only sprained. I decided never to do anything that stupid again. Of course, I have done many things just as stupid since then, and some even more so.

*

The Short and Tall Spies

There were strange informers living in Katmandu. The gossip that flew around town was even thicker than the dust. A rumor had it that Communist spies were after us, trying to hinder the progress of our expedition. The Chinese were engaged in dam construction, and, supposedly, we would probably be unable to find enough porters to carry our luggage. Our local friends whispered: "The spies are disguised as news reporters. One of them is very tall and the other one, very short; they're working as a team."

The little man our friends fingered as a reporter-spy looked as if he'd been borrowed from the Salvation Army. His Chinese uniform looked like a left over from the Long March, and he always loitered near the Japanese team members, a big smile on his face. On top of that, he and the tall spy were always taking pictures of each other with an Instamatic camera from Kodak, the most capitalistic company in that capitalist country, the United States. Maybe they stole the camera from the American spies, God knows! I wonder how they focused the camera, because they held it so close to each other's faces as they gritted their teeth and grinned. Perhaps a spy has to do everything this way, even taking photographs.

The tall one disguised himself as an Indian, although he didn't wear a turban. He had a great beard, and he wore the kind of dark sunglasses that you can't see through. He even wore those sunglasses at night and in the hotel. He probably thought he was invisible.

Don-chan cautioned me to be very careful when I talked to them. I went out of my way to tell them that I didn't have a Red Chinese visa, so in case I was blown off the South Col into Tibet, I would be delighted to say hello to Mao Tse-tung if they arrested me. I also told them I would love to ski down the mountains of Tibet or the Tien Shan mountains or the Amne Machin in China. They licked the ends of their pencils, asking me if they could write this down in their notes. I wondered if there were such things as very dumb and human spies. Anyway, in a few days, despite the rumor, we were able to get about eight hundred porters to come to our caravan starting point at the Lamsang Bridge. The construction site of the Red Chinese dam seemed rather empty that day.

*

While we had run around Tokyo dreaming of dirigibles, the clearheaded mountaineers already knew that we'd be accompanying the caravan on foot. They had spent six months making up detailed plans and had already begun shipping luggage to Nepal. Even with these careful preparations, there were a number of accidents. A seedy manufacturer supplied tent supports that broke down under a summer beach breeze; within a week, members of our caravan were snoring inside tents which had collapsed around them. And we had some accidents caused by broken crampons. Food especially was a fiasco. For instance, at one lunch we were scheduled to have sugar biscuits with canned sweet red beans and liquid sugar candy—some lunch!

*

The Real Expedition Begins

Once we crossed the Lamsang Bridge we said good-by to civilization. But what was civilization anyway? If it meant chrome, steel, concrete, and plastic, and all the noise and dirt and pollution, I preferred to say good-by.

If I needed any reminders of civilization, I had my parachute and a massive array of equipment to wear: a small oxygen tank, a helmet with a receiver in it, a jet pilot's oxygen mask, a microphone, and a life jacket.

*

Just letting the mind wander, freely exploring whatever attracts it, is the privilege of the person who has little to do. Although I was a captain, I had only one follower. He was the one who always answered the telephone at home, "Yes, this is the follower Tadano." He was the dependent of our family, a permanent guest, a very healthy, vigorous kind of person. His first name, Naotaka, means in Japanese, "Have you recovered?" Since his name unavoidably associated him with injury, we renamed him "Tak" Tadano.

A captain needs at least one follower. If you have many in the entourage, then it is too much trouble; you have to remember all the names. For a captain with one follower,

there was not much for me to do. When I wanted
something, I just called, "Hey, Tak!"

With someone like me for a captain, the team leaders,
like Tonko and Amma, had a lot to do. Some ran around
like shepherds herding sheep. Others continually lectured
the porters in a mixture of English, Sherpa, and Japanese.
Some team members oversaw the handling and tagging of
hundreds of crates that first morning of the trip.

There must have been about a thousand people milling
around. All the luggage had to be divided among eight
hundred porters. It looked like a small mountain; Sherpa
tents were nested in between those great piles of
equipment. Cooking smoke rose from the kitchen tents and
spread a choking haze over all the commotion. I was
reminded of the bazaars in Katmandu.

*

Unusual Expedition

Taisuke was chief in command, but we didn't know
how to describe his position or translate it into English for
the Sherpas, so everybody decided to give him the title of
general manager. "You don't really mean that he's going to
Mount Everest with you?" an incredulous reporter from the
Associated Press at Katmandu had asked when he saw fat
Taisuke. I heard this story from Ishihara, who was the home
overseer of the expedition and also a very young politician
in the Japanese Diet. Actually Ishihara was envious, because
originally he had planned to take leave of the National Diet
and go along with the Japan Mount Everest Ski Expedition
as commander-in-chief. We were all looking forward to it,
but the National Diet would not permit it. Since Japanese
always complain about government policies, we said to him:
"Forget all that bureaucratic trivia. Why don't you just come
anyway? You could play hooky!" However, I suppose it was
not so simple to just sneak away for a month.

Ishihara told me he used to walk a lot while he was a

student; he even tried to walk from Tokyo to Osaka, and he roamed the mountains for many days without eating or drinking. He was a sportsman, a soccer player, sailor, and writer, tall and handsome. As a politician, he became one of the new hopes of Japan when he won his election by three million votes. I didn't know him very well, but after spending some time with him, I felt that he was the most masculine of all men. He was not a mere political creation of the mass media. He was a man, not just an image. If the expedition was a success, I, Miura, would become a famous figure; of course, it would not be just me, but the team and the Japanese people as a nation. But if it failed, Ishihara would be asked, "Why did you take the job as titular head of this ridiculous expedition?" He would end up with the responsibility and the blame. He had nothing to gain and plenty to lose, but still he expended great effort speaking in our behalf to the diplomats of Japan and Nepal and our supporters at home. I really came to value the friendship of this fine man.

*

This Everest expedition was something very unusual for the Japanese people, attempting to achieve multiple objectives instead of just one. It was an ad hoc gathering of many young professionals, few of whom knew each other by name—professional film makers, skiers, mountaineers, scholars, doctors, professional photographers, writers, and journalists. Naturally, there were occasional antagonisms and disagreements, what with the constant dangers of wasting a great deal of time and also possibly losing one's life. We were taking a strenuous road. We carefully watched the project's development and were in turn watched with great concern. Even disbandment might have been appropriate. I don't know whether anybody else was considering failure, but I had to include it in our plans as a possibility because the whole thing was so fragile and uncertain.

Still the warmth and kindheartedness of people became

more obvious the further we went along. The more difficulties we had, the closer we grew to each other. That gave us new strength and power. By trusting each other completely and letting our lives depend on each other, we attained a great concentration of power and energy.

*

The primary thing when you take a sword in your hands is your intention to cut the enemy, whatever way you can. Whenever you parry, hit, spring, strike, or touch the enemy's sword, you must cut him in the same movement. If you think only of hitting, springing, striking, or touching the enemy, you will never be able to actually cut him. Only the intention to cut will achieve the cut.

MUSASHI "Ring of Water"

*

No Weak Followers Under a Strong Leader

From the beginning, no one ever predicted that our trip was even remotely possible; on the contrary, I heard that foreign journalists in Katmandu were surprised and amused. It was a logical response. Just look at our symbol—roly-poly Taisuke. None of our members looked very professional as expeditionists—all were a little bit on the heavy side. You could sense a trace of intelligence, but that was about all. The leaders were all in their thirties, but most of the team members were in their twenties. Observers predicted that we would not last three days, as if they looked forward to our collapse.

Taisuke reconfirmed his resolution to personally lead the expedition to Everest. The sad thing was that when he tried to put on his climbing knickers, he couldn't get them over his stomach—they would not stay up. He had to call out, "Are there any that are extra extra large?" Taisuke wore a big, brimmed hat he had bought at the bazaar in Katmandu that supposedly had belonged to a Gurkha soldier, a red sports shirt probably given to him by some bar girl in Ginza, a cheap pair of sneakers, and he carried a black umbrella instead of a walking stick—he was not the usual professional expedition commander.

*

"Let's go!" Don-chan roared. The great line of cargo started to move. It was much worse than Ali Baba and the forty quarreling thieves. Our eight hundred porters, with rags around their bodies, looked like *kumosuke*, ancient Japanese thieves who, having gathered their loot, tried to escape in their bare feet.

The line lurched forward in chaotic, ragtag confusion. I couldn't figure out why everybody was in such a hurry till I noticed that there were very few rocks or tree roots along the roadside for resting. Everyone was rushing ahead in order to find a resting place. It was like trying to get a seat in a commuter train. Since I had no intention of taking part in this competition, I ambled along with Taisuke and decided to take a nap at the edge of a small river at Lamsang, where the tents had been pitched. However, the tents had already been dismantled and carried away. It was too early; we had had breakfast only half an hour before. It was seven o'clock, and both of us were tired already.

*

People in Nepal cultivate their fields in a series of terraces, a stepladder for a giant to come down from heaven. You could see the long line of porters, like an army of ants, trailing through the fields, heading toward the sky. It was like being in Gulliver's world, watching the line of Lilliputians climbing the steps up the giant's knees.

*

Bala Bala Puts Up a Good Fight

When I awakened from my nap, there was no one around. I was alone in a lonely world. The noise and commotion of the bazaar had disappeared. "Quick! After them, before you get lost," I thought. Outside a little village, the road split in three directions. I debated which way to go. Not even five minutes after I had started, I was confused. I felt ridiculous, until I spotted some porters who had also stopped to rest just five minutes after starting up.

After an hour of slow, steady climbing, I reached a

little straw-roofed shack in the middle of the slope. Porters were gathered around drinking and making lots of noise. This was the equivalent of a drive-in, a bar and grill on this foot-sore freeway to Everest. From this restaurant, this little shack with a single charcoal burner stove, a friend called out excitedly: "I didn't know, but I kept drinking what they told me, and now I'm totally soused. This is the Nepalese equivalent of Japanese sake, and it sure is good." He offered me some *raksi* and *chang*, but I figured it was a little too early; I'd probably get tipsy. It was only a little after nine o'clock in the morning, so instead I asked for black tea. If things continued this way, I wondered when, or if, we would ever get to Everest. Before sundown I reached the tent site for our first night's stop. I was too tired to ask the name.

*

"He may not come at all, but if he doesn't make it he will have died trying," I thought. Finally, Taisuke heaved himself into camp, panting and dragging his feet. He collapsed in our tent, a mountain of sweat-soaked cloth and flesh.

I discovered during the fall scouting trip that nothing in this world is quite as cold-hearted as a caravan. Everybody just keeps walking, climbing, going up and down the hills, resting, walking, climbing without saying a word—walking, walking. A caravan in the Himalayas is a walking monster that never looks back. If you are left behind, the walking monster will just keep moving. Among mountaineers in Japan the custom is to keep pace with the weakest person when climbing. In other words, we start our first step with the spirit of helping each other. The people in this country—I wonder if they've fled from wolves and abominable snowmen too long, or if they still remember the time when they were chased by cannibals with sticks and spears. The weak ones who fall out, die; only the strong ones survive. The Nepalese walk as if nature had taught them, and they remain loyal to that teaching. Since we

Overlooking the Khumbu glacier and the valleys below. *Photo copyright © Kazunari Yasuhisa.*

Setting the world ski altitude record. *Photo copyright © Kazunari Yasuhisa.*

My chute was like a useless toy balloon. *Photo copyright © Akira Kotani.*

Speeding toward the Bergschrund. *Photo copyright © Kazunari Yasuhisa.*

Sacred Buddhist "Mani" stones. *Photo copyright © Akira Kotani.*

Skiing on Shangri-la glacier. *Photo copyright © Akira Kotani.* ➤

Japanese were now mingled with this great, moving mass, the rules we used to follow did not apply. Once you enter into the stream of charging animals, you have to match their pace.

The caravan raised massive clouds of dust. By the end of each day we looked like coal miners or rice planters. I could accept my outside being dirty, but not my insides. I was determined to eat nutritious, natural food. Preservatives, artificial coloring, and artificial flavoring were out of the question. I didn't want those poisons in my system in the high altitudes of Mount Everest, so I gave the Sherpas and the porters all the canned and freeze-dried food that I had brought from Japan. Instead, I ate potatoes and *tsamba*—a flour made out of burnt barley, a traditional Sherpa food. One day I was able to get some ghee (yak butter) at a little place we called "the coffee shop of the mountain pass." I put that package of yak butter in my pocket along with the seaweed which my friends from northern Japan had sent me and ate as I walked.

I felt that eating ghee was the greatest nutritional idea I had had for a long time. So I transferred the rapidly melting butter to a plastic bag and put it in the pouch of my backpack. Whenever it was time to rest, I ate this stuff, and because it made me thirsty, I drank water out of the creek. In a very short while, I experienced the most vicious diarrhea.

I began to feel worried and depressed. I had already done so many wrong things. All these mistakes, and we hadn't even reached the foot of the mountain—what would I do to myself next?

*

Strong, Still Center
    When both you and the enemy attack at the same moment, hit with your body, hit with your spirit, and hit from the Void. From utter stillness accelerate to maximum power.

MUSASHI "Ring of Water"

*

Yoga Breathing

The grass terrace on the mountaintop where we stayed last night had a name—*Pakka. Baka,* a similar-sounding word in Japanese, means "stupid" or "dumb," so everybody agreed we were a bunch of dummies as we started on our way. Since we were on the higher part of the mountain, the scenery was supposed to be good, but it was cloudy. We couldn't even see the great white peaks.

*

Time passed like overflowing milk. As I climbed, putting each foot on the earth, I began to feel very happy. I felt as if I were surrounded by God and invisible angels. I was climbing easily. Even the air felt soft around me, and I felt holy, as if many spirits were carrying me.

*

Dynamic breath equals good conditioning. My breathing had become so powerful that I could blow away the dust and the leaves at the side of the road. *Dynamic Breath* was the title of a pamphlet that I received from a Hindu ascetic when I visited New Delhi last year. It was printed on very poor paper, but there were some good suggestions in it. I had knocked on the door of a Yogi's hut one evening at sunset. A dark-skinned man in a white shirt appeared and asked me suddenly in English, "What do you think Yoga is?" I replied that that was what I wanted to find out. He took me inside and told me he was already closing for the day. "But you can come tomorrow, and, meanwhile, why don't you read this pamphlet?" he said, handing me *Dynamic Breath.* Unfortunately, I had to leave on the airplane heading for Katmandu the next day. When I told him so, I also mentioned that I was going to Everest and asked him to teach me one thing. He told me to breathe the goodness of the galaxy: "Exhale the bad things within yourself and inhale love. That's what's written in this pamphlet, so take your time and read it." I asked him, "How much do you ask in return?" and he replied: "Oh no, please don't! I should thank you for visiting me." There are still some real men in India. From that pamphlet I realized that powerful breathing begins with the exhale.

*

When I started breathing consciously, I went to extremes. When the path leveled off, I forgot about it. But when I started to climb, and especially when I found my breath short, I remembered. On the dusty, climbing road and on the steep hills my breathing became so intense that the dust flew around me when I exhaled. It was not such a big thing, but counting the leaves that spun around me because of my breathing kept me from getting bored while I walked. Of course, I was doing this to train my lungs, to prepare myself for the uphill trip on the glacier, hoping that I would be able to breathe easily at an altitude of twenty-six thousand feet.

*

To Hit the Enemy "In a Single Timing"
"In a Single Timing" means, when you have closed with the enemy, hit him as quickly and as directly as possible when you see that he is still undecided. Without moving your body or settling your spirit, time your hit to coincide with his moment's indecision between withdrawing or attacking.
You must train to achieve this timing.

MUSASHI "Ring of Water"

*

The Second Prime of My Life

We arrived at a little place called Suruke. *Suruka* means "Shall we do it!" in Japanese. So we all said, "Shall we do it!" and decided to take naps. The careless joy of my nap was similar to the long-forgotten beginnings of love, before I had known suffering and sorrow.

How can I express this? I walk all day and grow very tired. But each day it feels different. I change with my surroundings. I have been exhausted many times before from sports and mountain climbing, but it always felt like a heavy stiffness, as if my body had been soaked in vinegar.

But on this route to Mount Everest, after everything is

over for the day, after eating, talking with friends, after listening to a cassette tape, after finishing everything, I crawl into my sleeping bag, and my body, each cell of my body, starts to sing very softly and starts to expand in joy and happiness and warmth, like a spring field under soft sunlight, or like yeasted bread dough starting to rise. My body starts to relax; my heart rides on the clouds, singing a song of wonder. I know I will have a sweet dream.

I wonder if this is the prime of life. Is this the springtime, the prime time, just at the age when I am no longer green and hard and suffering—no longer young? Was youth just a label and age a mirage? At thirty-seven, I was no longer young—I was into my middle age. For years I had felt that something had already collapsed and that maybe it was too late for great, physical challenges. But with a clock, if you wind it up again, the time passes by unchanged. This trek to Everest was rewinding my clock. Though the hands did not turn back, the spring rewound to vigorous strength.

It was night. Listening to the trickling sound of the creek, looking at the starlight that came through the crack of the tent, I fell asleep.

*

A clear day. I decided to call this walking up and down the mountain road with a backpack "heavy marathon walking." Surrounded by the porters, my "barefooted angels," I thought the caravan had become almost pleasant.

The caravan was something of a holiday for the porters. We were paying and feeding them to leave their homes and wander the mountains with us.

Some porters lazed around a lime tree by the water, opening up lunch, drinking happily, singing, even dancing from time to time. When they got tired of laughter, they put their packs on their backs once more and started walking again. Coughing a little, talking a little, smeared with sweat, and panting, they trudged toward the next patch of shade. Probably all the caravans of antiquity stopped at this same

Hardworking porter takes a break. *Photograph copyright © Akira Kotani.*

place, drank the same water, and carried on their own festivities.

How many times I was saved from depression by their happy singing during this long, strenuous journey! The atmosphere of freedom and spontaneity in them and the pride of being wild, even their wearing rags, made me aware of the value, the preciousness, of living close to nature. They were employees but not slaves.

In the evening I sat down to contemplate. I came to feel alive after emptying all the pockets of my mind. The awareness started in my legs, which were set like Buddha, on the earth. *I am a child of earth. I feel a great root in the earth. I feel that I'm living proudly, and from my roots set deep in the soil, my mind expands into galactic space, predicting a quiet self-revolution within me.*

*

The Fire and Stones Cut
   In single combat, when the enemy's sword and your own sword clash with equal force, cut through with utter concentration, neither raising, lowering, nor withdrawing your sword even a little. All your forces—legs, body and hands—are focused along the cutting edge of your sword.
   MUSASHI "Ring of Water"

*

On the Move

Clear sky. More than clear, the sky was truly pure—absolutely no clouds. It was very dry among the dusty fields baked by the sunlight in this subtropical zone. All the water in the rice field had evaporated, but along the road there were blossoming rhododendrons and cacti and banana trees. We passed a funeral in the morning; the sad song of distant mourning was succeeded by a wedding parade at noon, with laughter and blaring trumpets. In the afternoon, toward evening, we passed one more wedding, accompanied by the sound of gunshots. I napped at a little village in a mountain pass where we had tried, unsuccessfully, to buy a pig. After drinking the Sherpa's alcoholic concoctions, *raksi* and *chang*, I fell fast asleep.

*

I got up in a hurry and ran after the caravan. Once I found my pace, I felt in good condition, very refreshed. Even when I ran out of breath, even when I felt tired enough to collapse, my legs, independent of my lungs, could still walk lightly. I caught up with the caravan and passed it and made it to the next camp with hours to spare.

*

Taisuke said the campsite looked like one out of the California gold rush. One thousand people: porters, Sherpas, Japanese, all sprawled across a barren, terraced field among scattered piles of gear. This camp was certainly different from the one we had enjoyed the day before, when we listened to the water, surrounded by lime trees on the hills, soft grass, and marvelous scenery. This camp was not romantic at all, but, then, it seemed more lively.

*

After dinner, I took an evening walk on the road to a *chorten*—a little Tibetan prayer house by the roadside. I sat down to contemplate the night. I turned my back on the lights and gay commotion of the campfires and faced the line of black peaks edged in starlit snow. I closed my eyes and melted right into the void. *This is a very important moment. Just let the mind go free. Consciousness encircles itself.*

I returned to the tent and started to write a letter I wasn't sure I would ever mail. I wrote it listening to some Brazilian jazz on the cassette tape. I was sorry I hadn't brought Rachmaninoff's Piano Concerto no. 2 and also "White Lovers"—a winter Olympics song. So many things that I forgot to bring, and none of it mattered.

Dear Tomoko,
   I have been taking the road to Everest step by step, and I'm full of a strange happiness. That is because there are many angels surrounding me as I climb. I'm supported by their kindly spirits. There seem to be a tremendous number of them crowding around, but at times just one—a kind of all embracing unity—I don't really know. It feels as though

someone or something is protecting and encouraging me. This is the first time I've experienced anything like this. In this world of Everest, even to run out of breath, or to sweat, or strain with effort—everything makes me feel happy. Every step is taking me to a wonderful world.

I never finished the letter.

*

"Today's course will be a very long and tiring one," said Don-chan. Though I felt a little tired, I added some weight to my backpack. I decided to test my endurance. In excellent condition, I caught up with the kitchen boys at the next camp as they ran around looking for a place to settle.

*

The campsite was on a river bank. I jumped naked into an ice-cold stream with Tak and a couple of friends. It was freezing. I was amazed that none of us had a heart attack. We slept naked on the warm beach sand. Napping in the afternoon sun, we listened to a Spaghetti Western theme song, "Gunman of the Sunset." We watched the sunlight reflecting patterns on the stream as if it were a movie screen, playing out the images the music brought to mind.

*

Glue and Lacquer Body
    The spirit of the glue and lacquer body is to stick to the enemy and not separate from him, whether he attacks or retreats. When you approach the enemy, stick to him firmly with your head, body, and legs. People tend to lead with their head and legs while their bodies lag shyly behind. You should stick so firmly that there is not the slightest gap between your body and the enemy's.

MUSASHI "Ring of Water"

*

Trouble as Usual

Blisters were inevitable. I thought I was cautious enough. I was wearing mountain-climbing shoes that I'd been breaking in since last year. The pack was kind of heavy, but it was the way I walk—half running—that did it to me. I noticed a strange pain in my heel, and sure enough, late one afternoon, there was a great big double blister, all puffed up and purple. I got some iodine, a needle, cotton, and some thread from the doctor. Remembering how my father used to clean blisters with a needle, I punctured the wound and squeezed the water out. I left the iodine-coated thread inside the blister and trimmed away the rest of the protruding thread. It was supposed to heal in one night, but it took four because I walked on it every day. It was a rather primitive operation.

*

March 11. Because of the snow and sleet, the wind was very cold, but I climbed in my usual shorts. My legs grew cold. I felt as though all my energy was draining out at my knees. I ignored my weakness because my lungs seemed to be in good condition. No matter how short of breath I got, my heart never tired. The air felt a little lighter and seemed to pass through my lungs with ease. My blister still bothered me, so I used my sneakers. I was told that the mountain course for today would be a short one, but we hiked beside the river for an hour, then climbed up a steep mountain pass for three hours, and finished with an hour of downhill. It snowed. We felt sorry for the barefooted angels—the porters; we were concerned that some of them might run away, but they tromped merrily through the snow and brought all the gear to camp before nightfall.

*

I got to the next day's camp too early again. Two hundred yards from the campsite was a food hut with a thatched roof. "All right, I'm chartering the whole place today." I drank *chang* and *raksi* and ate duck eggs. I drank and I drank, and I ate and I ate, and I invited in all the people who passed by. After three hours of continuous drinking and eating, the restaurant ran out of liquor and eggs. I don't think I have ever been so happy and drunk.

Raksi and *chang*, the local liquors of Nepal, are full of laughter. They expand my mind, and I become a child of earth and heaven. They speak of happy spring days, of the strong sun of summer, of the autumn day that changes into loneliness, and of the freezing winter days that come after that.

*

The famous Sherpa Girmi Dorje said once that when the snow comes thick, there's bound to be trouble. In 1963, the American expedition encountered snow up to their chests at Pheriche, and they had to use yaks to send the luggage down to a lower elevation.

We heard that the Japanese Alpine Club team which was preceeding us with its great quantity of equipment, was having severe problems with snow. Many of the porters were dropping their loads and deserting.

*

We saw a Cessna flying out of Lukla Airport, heading for Katmandu. Though we were not headed that way, we wistfully watched its effortless flight.

*

There were nights when I could not fall asleep, and there were days when I was absolutely exhausted. But still we walked and walked so as not to be left behind. Even with diarrhea and fevers, we followed gamely.

*

If you looked carefully, you could see the enormous effort that people like Don-chan, Tonko, the young mountaineers, and the Sherpas had really put in. It was a tremendous amount of work organizing all the baggage for eight hundred porters. And switching porters every three days, as new villagers were pressed into service and old ones dropped out to return to their fields, was an incredibly complex problem in backwoods politics.

The porters were mostly farmers from the villages that we passed along the way. Each group was organized by a *naike,* or chief—usually the oldest and most important man of the village. He would decide who to put where, and then his people would carry the luggage.

The problem was, all these villages were so small that we had a hard time getting even thirty porters from any one settlement. We had so much baggage that we needed at least eight hundred people; in most cases, all the families of the village would participate, even old men, women, and children. Their pay was about a dollar per day, and they provided their own food and lodging. If they were from a nearby village, they were usually able to stay over at their neighbors' houses, but those who came from far away, like those who joined the party at the beginning, had to walk around with their food and their bedding on top of their packs for more than a week. At night, the temperature went down to about ten degrees Fahrenheit, but they huddled in between the rocks and slept peacefully till the first colors of dawn called them to their labors.

They were divided into two categories: high porters and low porters. At Namche Bazar, the porters who came from above Namche all usually went barefoot, and even on the rocky mountain roads they usually hung their shoes from their packs. The low porters came from low altitudes, and were not accustomed to snow.

*

It was very tiring, this long, long journey. One day I had cramps in my legs, and my body felt like lead, and the songs of the angels had turned into grunts. In my speed-skiing days I was described as "the man who doesn't run, he flies." But today I couldn't even overtake a cow that had passed me by. The spring morning sunshine that we enjoyed when we first started to climb to Lamsang had felt like the beginnings of love, and the angel dance encouraged us. But the love went cold as we grew weary. We had come very far.

*

The Flowing Water Cut
     When struggling blade-to-blade with the enemy, and he withdraws to spring with his long sword, fill the space between you with your own sword, expand your body and spirit and cut him slowly, following his withdrawal. Though you can cut with certainty with this technique, you must discern your enemy's ability, lest he draw you into a trap.
                                        MUSASHI "Ring of Water"

*

We Have Come a Long Way

Crossing the snowy pass we dropped into a red flower forest of rhododendron. And in the village below, the full blooms of peach and plum blossoms festooned the trees. The long caravan of barefooted angels continued. I wondered why they were resting so much. Even the angels were tired.

Bistali, bistali, ("slowly, slowly"). Some of them stopped and rested after only five minutes of slow climbing. It became a very difficult task for them too, teetering on bare feet, toes digging into the mud. Children held on, carrying luggage that looked twice as big as themselves. An old man climbed with a pack which must have been three times his size. I was impressed by the girls' endurance; along with their loads, some had little baskets on top of their heads and a baby with great big eyes inside.

*

I wondered if they learned it from the snails. On top of the luggage each porter carried a little ragged bag in which there were pots and pans and spoons, potatoes, sugar, salt, pepper, *tsamba, chang,* and *raksi.* They dug out miraculous assortments of things, like magicians. Their bedding looked like a few pieces of rags, but when the cold night came, they bundled up in it, and, as if they had melted into the mud, they fell soundly to sleep. And during the day, no matter how tired they were or how slowly they staggered up the trail, a few moments' rest, and they looked happier.

We were a long, long freight train with legs. Perhaps a local train, and the stations were those *chang* and *raksi* drive-ins.

The little tea shops with the thatched roofs were mostly made out of branches and twigs. When climbing a long, hard pass, as soon as I wished for a tea shop, there it was. Each restaurant was equipped with about five chipped cups, and everyone had to wait his turn. We heard the tinkling of coins and all the noise and commotion. Then after a few moments, a voice would call out, *"Tsaina, tsaina,"* which

Women porters carried their children on their heads as well as 50–70 pound loads on their backs. *Photograph copyright © Akira Kotani.*

means "the end." Everything had been sold. Closed for the day. It seemed as if they went out of business until the next caravan came along. Those who did not get to drink rushed on to the next stop. Just like in a "civilized" country.

*

Though the next camp was located at a height of ten thousand feet, my morning pulse was fifty-five and I felt great. I started about one hour after everybody had left and took only half the projected three hours marching time to get to the lunch stop. I caught up and reached the head of the line. On the downhill I was cautious not to strain my knee. One Sherpa, Ang Pema, who used to be a Gurkha soldier, raced with me about halfway down, but I think he gave up, even though my pack was heavier. I had put on my mountain-climbing shoes for a change. The blister had hardened.

*

I began to feel that my climbing boots were kicking the earth violently and disrespectfully.

The barefooted angels have the most elegant way of walking on this earth. Civilized Japanese feet are thin, like old worn slippers, and they are getting worse; they are only able to stand or walk on *tatami*, grass mats, carpeting, or sandy beaches. When I put on mountain-climbing shoes, suddenly they started to kick the earth. I preferred sneakers. On this mountain road where the flowers were blooming and the grass was green, I felt like walking gently, softly. The feeling takes me back to when I was just an animal, a thousand lifetimes and a million memories ago.

*

They're such strange, happy drinks: *chang* and *raksi*. They are supposed to be the ancestors of Japanese rice wines. But when they get into my bloodstream, all the cells in my body start dancing and singing. The cameraman Otaki caught a cold and diarrhea. Probably he won too much money playing *dobon*, a local gambling game that became popular among the expedition people. Don-chan said he'd never seen so many drunks in an expedition team before. Tonko, the doctor, Ohba, Soga, the Sherpa porters, *bala bala sabu,* and *bala sabu*—they all were drinking too much. Whenever we found a little "drive-in" along the way, we drank like horses and then resumed walking. Our reasoning was that since you get more tired walking after drinking, it amounted to harder training, which would make us stronger by constant repetition.

*

Sherpa Girls

Under the starlight around the campfire, a Sherpa dance began. The lovely village girls were a little shy as they all touched shoulders in a circle. Bright angels with rags—maybe they lived a little closer to heaven, or a little closer to the sun. They had a bright shine in their eyes. Our Japanese gaiety looked like a dance, but it seethed with more primitive violence.

The Sherpani—Sherpa girls—who grew up in this elegant flow of time, were laughing. They kept time with their feet, quietly but very passionately, repeating the rhythms like waves. They danced and sang in rings, their shoulders locked together. The moon rose among the stars.

If they didn't get back to camp by ten o'clock at night, the expedition team members had to pay twenty rupees ($3.00), and the Sherpas had to pay ten rupees ($1.50) for punishment. There was a lot of payment that night.

*

The men crawled out of their tents at the sound of the breakfast whistle. They all looked as if the morning were too bright. The money that was collected as a penalty was saved to buy more *chang* and *raksi* for everybody—a vicious circle.

*

Taisuke's Miracle

March 25. It was 2:30 in the morning. I had gotten up to urinate, and I could not go back to sleep. The Sherpa night

Dancing with the Sherpa girls. *Photograph copyright © Akira Kotani.*

watchman was stoking the campfire. I asked him in a combination of Sherpa and English whether he had some tea, and he answered, "Making, sir." But I felt sorry to bother him, so I drank some water and went back to the tent. I tried to fall asleep, but thinking about Taisuke's "miracle" kept me awake.

Yesterday we had a health checkup for the entire team and all the Sherpas, including a general examination and an electrocardiograph. Strangely, people who were known as first-class mountaineers, such as Amma, Otaki, Ohba, Kotani, and the young men of Ishihara Productions—in other words, those whose jobs and pleasure took them to the mountains and to nature, who had been trained to this kind of life since childhood—had headaches, colds, symptoms of mountain sickness, hoarse voices, and slight fevers. We began to think it might be impossible to continue the trip without repeating last year's mistake in which one of the team members had come down with such a severe case of mountain sickness that he had to be lifted out by helicopter.

During the checkup we broke up into different groups according to condition and symptoms. The teams were ranked A, B, C, and D. Group A consisted of those who were supposed to rest for six days and who at this point displayed no compatibility with the high mountains. Those in group B had adapted a little better but were still plagued with severe afflictions. Group C needed about three days of careful watching. Group D were the iron men.

The most amazing thing was that fat Taisuke, the person for whom we were so concerned, was part of group D. Through my conditioning program, I had managed to put myself in group D, but I really belonged in group C because I still had diarrhea from eating that horrible ghee.

The doctor said, "Taisuke, you are a real rough, tough man."

*

This is what I entered in my diary about this day:

A man can train himself to become stronger, but even a strong man has weaknesses. The source of Taisuke's great vitality comes from fighting with the witches of midnight, nestling in the world's highest priced bars in smog-filled Tokyo. For him, a Himalayan trip is like visiting a country bar. The amount of energy that he spends on this trip is only equivalent to his output when he makes the rounds of bars in his hometown.

I have accompanied him to his nocturnal battlefields a few times on the Ginza, but the amount of alcohol that he consumed and his strange women and food made me feel like a little rabbit, and I was completely exhausted by midnight.

Those men of the night are the tough ones: they may seem weak, but they pack two days into one, night and day, 365 days a year. You are the stronger ones, oh you men of midnight, you are the mountain people, you are the sportsmen, you are fighting great battles day and night repeatedly, which bear no comparison with other worldly adventures.

On reflection, I couldn't believe this diary entry. I must have been completely out of my mind, suffering symptoms of mountain sickness. At least Taisuke had changed. He had lost a little weight, his beard had grown, and his large eyes even had more shine; he seemed like a reincarnation of Prince Shotoku Taishi, whose picture appears on Japanese money. I thought that Taisuke's photograph would be good enough to be a model for counterfeit bills.

*

According to Don-chan, our team must be the weakest in the history of Everest expeditions. Come to think of it, only about half of the team had ever been to the mountains; the others were Ishihara's cameramen, who said they had been to Mount Fuji or to the Japanese Alps, but when asked about it, all they could say was "Wow, what trouble we had on big, tough Mount Fuji." Most of them had never even experienced winter mountains in Japan without ski lifts. Don-chan himself was still limping from a knee injury he had suffered on a ski-training trip last winter; he crashed into a trash can at a local resort.

Two-thirds of the expedition team had colds and sore throats. We sounded like a campsite of crows. I don't think there ever was an expedition that drank so much. I have never seen such a team; they stopped and drank every chance they got.

*

The Disappearance of a Chicken Boy

The caravan's day started with a kitchen boy, a young Sherpa, calling out at 6:00 in the morning, "Serve, tea sir." Last year there was the incident of the disappearing kitchen boy. Tonko, one of Japan's foremost mountaineers, who had graduated with honors from a famous university, spoke better Sherpa dialect than English. Trying to be friendly with the Sherpas, he drank too much *chang* and *raksi*. He crawled into the sleeping bag next to me in the middle of the night and mumbled for a while, and then suddenly he shouted, "Hey, chicken boy, chicken boy, *eto, eto, awa, wee,* tomorrow morning, do you understand?" Shortly, we heard an answer from the Sherpa boy sleeping nearby. When I asked Tonko what he had just said, he said he had told the Sherpa, "Tomorrow morning we want to eat our breakfast at eight o'clock." The first *eto* meant "eight," and the next *eto* meant "eat," and by the next two words, *awa* and *wee,* he meant to say "we," but had forgotten how, so he had decided to say both "our" and "we." I was impressed that the Sherpa had understood what he had said—until the next morning. When we found that the kitchen boy was missing, we were quite concerned, but then he appeared, dirty, sweating, and gripping chickens in both hands. We finally realized that Tonko had called the kitchen boy a "chicken" boy. The lad thought we wanted to eat chickens for breakfast, so he had been running all over the local village looking for them. From then on, he was called chicken boy instead of kitchen boy, and we were able to eat fresh chicken every day. However, when we encountered some of the expedition members who had been behind us, they complained that they could find no eggs for sale in any of the villages.

*

Many Enemies
When you are fighting one against many, draw both long sword and companion sword and take a wide-stretched left and wide-stretched right posture. Your spirit must expand and embrace your opponents. Even though they attack from all four directions, you must chase them. Waiting is bad. Observe the attacking order, and go to meet those who attack first. Sweep your eyes across your enemies, observe the varying stages of readiness. Attack the foremost, cutting left and right alternately with your swords. Always re-assume your posture of readiness on both sides. Cut the enemies down as they advance, crushing them in the direction from which they come. You must draw your attackers together, like tying a sheaf of rice or a catch of fish. When they are piled up with no room to move, cut them down.

MUSASHI "Ring of Water"

*

Barefooted Angels

Two weeks passed before we reached the area of the great snowfall. There was almost no snow left, only little remnants of white in the shade of the steep slope. The strangest thing happened; the porters who wore canvas shoes all took them off when they came to the snow. I guess they trusted their bare toes for traction more than those old worn-out tennis shoes.

For training purposes, I carried as much as the porters—fifty or sixty pounds. Thus I could understand how they suffered under their loads. I joined their chorus of panting while walking and climbing.

These Himalayan expeditions are possible only because of the strength and endurance of these mountain people, these barefooted tribesmen who were born to walk and walk to live.

*

I thought as I climbed, "How many mountains and rivers must I pass to reach Everest, the lonesome end of the

The porters' bare feet were tough; they trod over stones, mud and snow as easily as we did in our boots. *Photograph copyright © Akira Kotani.*

earth?" But the climbing was really not so bad, because we were so well rewarded by the scenery. I let myself soak in the glacial beauty of the Himalayas that began to appear before us. I walked down the path by the creek with a happy feeling, and crossed a somewhat unsteady suspension bridge. I imagined the blacksmith of the village carefully pounding his anvil and tending the bellows, making this bridge, a long time ago. The canyon was not very big, only about 160 feet wide, and the bridge swung 25 feet above the icy waters.

The bridge collapsed the next day. I was having lunch with two reporters from the Yomiuri newspaper, at the huge rock terrace by the creek, when an old porter came and said, "Bridge *tsaina*, sir." According to a Sherpa interpreter, the bridge had fallen, and many, many people with it.

One Japanese reporter usually walked around with an umbrella as if it were a walking stick, in a contemplative manner, looking very elegant and refined. But this gentleman of the mountain ran like a rabbit at the first hint of a newsworthy story. He was a reporter, after all.

I swallowed the last tea from the thermos and went after the reporters. I thought that because I had been walking around with a heavy pack, I would be able to run much faster with nothing on my back, but I was wrong. I felt like a piece of heavy machinery with no oil as I walked stiff-legged toward the bridge.

I had imagined that the whole bridge had fallen, but actually, the chain on one end had worked loose and one side of the bridge was dangling close to the surface of the water. From the casual expressions on everyone's faces, I guessed that no one had drowned.

Tonko had been so weak with amoebic dysentery that he wasn't even able to drink his favorite liquor, but the moment he saw the bridge fall, he dove into the water to help the porters and retrieve the luggage.

While some of the porters stood around naked, wet and trembling, many of the village wives gathered, mumbling that their husbands were over on the other side of the bridge and would not be home until sundown. Since most of the men came home completely drunk, they would not notice that the bridge was down and probably fall in themselves.

*

Charming Chaos

Psychologically, I was completely exhausted after the bridge incident, so I had another lunch by the river with Don-chan and Tonko. Since I didn't have any more black tea left, I used icy water from the river to mix my mush of brown sugar and *tsamba*. The location was impressive; a snowy ridge loomed twelve thousand feet above us. I was tired, but I pressed on. Whenever I felt that I was too tired to move, I would think about the South Col, almost twenth-five thousand feet high. I kept telling myself it would be a lot more strenuous and painful up there. But no matter what I told myself, my breath was almost gone and my heart could not beat any faster. I felt I could last for another hour, maybe.

*

A place named Sete stood perched on a terrace above the clouds, a great sea of clouds. A Tibetan Buddhist temple clung to the side of the slope. We had thought that the stone fence around the temple terrace would provide an elegant campsite, but at sunset all the cows came home and lay down to sleep next to the fence, as if to tell us this was their home. We were very considerate of them as we ate our curried rice, until a cow stuck her head into the pot and a Sherpa had to yell and chase her away.

*

Leisurely following the caravan, I ran into a little girl standing barefoot in the snow, crying. She was a child of one of the porter families, waiting for her parents. It was her first time in snow, and she didn't know what to make of it. Her tough, calloused feet didn't hurt; she was just confused.

This mountain pass was where the porters had run off

in the great snow storm two weeks before. Some of our own complaining porters now fled too. The pass was very tough going, even for those wearing mountain boots. I had great difficulties today. I had forgotten to change out of my running shoes. They slipped in the snow and got soaking wet. However, a third of the downhill section had enough snow to glissade, and it was terrific. I skied on my smooth-soled shoes. My follower, Tak, was napping in the middle of the stretch, but when he saw me skimming over the snow, he joined in the fun. We burst into the village of Jumbesi, which lay in the gorge below. It looked right out of a Swiss postcard. We expected to hear an Alpenhorn any moment. At the far end of the gorge stood the great white mountain Nun Puhr, jutting 21,700 feet into the sky.

Endless plodding made me feel as though I were turning into a mindless machine, so I decided to do some calisthenics and wake up. I jumped back and forth five hundred times on the ski-training machine which I had brought. I hopped like a rabbit against the slopes about two hundred times, then finished off with push-ups. I was finally getting into shape.

*

"Tent *Tsaina!"*

Around eight o'clock, the wind grew stronger. In the tent next to us were the reporters from the Yomiuri papers and Tonko. Suddenly, I heard Tonko shouting in the windy dusk, "Hey there, Sherpa, tent *tsaina*, tent *tsaina*." The main support of the tent structure had broken in the wind. You could hear the sound of laughter around the tents. We joined in, enjoying someone else's misfortune. Then, our tent began to look suspicious, and the support on Taisuke's side suddenly broke. Yamada and Ohba, the equipment managers, apologized and changed the pole for us immediately, saying the cheap ones were no good. They decided to use the poles from the higher altitude tents. At the next strong gust, the support on my side broke off.

Because it was too much trouble, I decided to hell with it, and slept under the canvas.

The wind flapped the material in my face, and it was too noisy to sleep. I went outside, and saw that all the tents had the same problems, especially Kotani's; both supports on his tent were broken, but only one other man was awakened by the commotion. I could see him rummaging around with a flashlight under the translucent cloth. Most of the men were still sleeping, snoring, in swathes of nylon underneath the broken tent supports. They looked like a field of comic-book monsters.

I found out later that the name of this village— Jumbesi—meant "the crib of the moon." It was rather a wild crib for us, but after a few days, when I learned the meaning, the romantic name made me feel nostalgic, and I wrote a little story—a fairy story.

*

The Crib of the Moon

I feel a little embarrassed talking about fairy tales at my age. I feel embarrassed, not because I am telling a fairy tale, but because I had forgotten such things for so long a time, and felt the dryness of a heart in which the joys of childhood had long since turned to dust. I think it is true that our imaginations have been stifled by the complexities of modern living. Deep in the villages of the Himalayas I found a trace of what we lost a long time ago—the strangely mournful sounds of the village festivities and the feeling of kinship with life.

This is my story.

*

Once upon a time there was a poor little orphan baby in this village, deep, deep in the Himalayas, many mountains and canyons away from the capital. A long time ago, when people first started to live in the gorge, it was a really beautiful place. Even now it is quite beautiful, but at that time even the gods themselves were proud of this canyon and visited it often. The mountains were so high that the clouds could only manage to pass by their feet, and a cold wind blew almost all year round. When the winds grew tired from carrying the clouds, they would scatter dew to lighten their loads. The village was very poor and the people were barely able to grow enough food for themselves. It was difficult to raise a little baby.

In the far end of the gorge there was a mountain named Nun Puhr, which had protected people in the village from all their enemies for a long time. The mountain felt sorry for the baby, but because he was a mountain of cold snow and hard rock and was always fighting off strong winds and storms, he could not help care for the child. However, because the mountain reached so high up in the sky, he was able to talk to the stars, the moon, the sun, and the clouds any time he wanted to. He talked about the baby, but no one paid much attention. A star had offered some part-time care, but knowing how unreliable stars were, it was not much help. At that point, there was a pat on Nun Puhr's shoulder. "Would you like me to take care of the baby?" It was the moon, who had prepared herself for the job by leaving half of herself to the sun, making the rest of her just like a crib for the baby to sleep in.

The little baby disappeared from the village before anyone noticed; but the villagers did not think it had died, because every time they saw a crescent moon, they were able to find the little baby sleeping in the crib of the moon. It was then that they started to call their village Jumbesi.

*

It is really a simple little story, but it felt good to write.

*

The Rabbit That Lives on the Moon

There's a sparkling beauty in the eyes of the people who live in that cold and lonely village. Of course, there are those nonsensical drunken old men and some shifty-eyed young people. But this is only natural when there are so many people crowded together. I was very impressed by the loyalty and devotion they show each other, qualities that seem to be disappearing in the "civilized" world of today, but which still exist among these barefooted angels living in a forgotten corner of the Far East. Maybe the ancient myths of India had something to do with it. There's a story which represents their attitude toward service. It goes something like this:

*

How did a rabbit ever manage to live on the moon? Once upon a time, one of the greatest gods appeared in a village of animals, disguised as an old man and looking just like any Sherpa. When he came upon a monkey, a rabbit, and a fox, he said: "I have come a long way, and I don't know anybody around here. I have not eaten in many days. If you have something, please spare me some food." The monkey quickly climbed up a tree and plucked some nuts, and the fox ran off to catch some meat for the old man to eat. But the rabbit couldn't climb trees, and he didn't have sharp teeth. When he realized he could not get any food for the old man, the rabbit dove into the campfire and said, "Please eat me!" Everybody tried to stop him, but it was already too late, and the poor creature died. The god was very impressed and decided to honor the rabbit's devotion by letting him play forever on the pure and beautiful moon.

*

The Sherpas who grew up with this story, the people of the mountains of Nepal, have not forgotten its meaning. They are the most generous and self-effacing people in the world.

Taking the lead is one of the most important points of strategy. To do so, you must maximize the strength of your position, see through the enemy's spirit so that you grasp his strategy and defeat him. Taking the lead means accurately preceding the flow of events.

MUSASHI ''Ring of Fire''

4

Higher Altitudes

WHEN THE weather grew clear, it seemed as if the
mountains had lost their shyness. I felt that way every day,
under the clear blue, endless sky. The goddesses
surrounding the white throne of God stood tall. Every time
the wind blew away one of their cloudy veils, their white
and beautiful complexions came into view. The slopes,
towering over the black forest, seemed powerful
enough to preserve this valley's lonely privacy from
"civilized" intrusion.

*

In the evening, I exercised by jumping up and down
like a rabbit in the grassy area around the tent. The local
police commissioner and his family had accepted our
invitation to dine and had just arrived. I ran down to meet
them. In his youth, the commissioner had been a soccer
player, and he was pleased with the way I greeted him. He
asked me how old I was, and when I told him thirty-seven,
he replied that I only looked twenty-seven. Even if it was

just a word of kindness, it made me very happy. I wanted to believe it, so I thanked him.

*

The liaison officer, Mr. Rai, said he had worked many times for foreign expeditions as a communications officer but had never seen a man so strong as me. I was still not as strong as I hoped to be, but was pleased by his comment anyway.

During the marches the Sherpas looked at me with patronizing eyes. When I ran through them like the wind, loaded with my own luggage just like a porter, I guess they were trying to tell me not to work too hard. "Once I reach the glaciers I may take it easy, but for now, I will push myself to the limit," I told myself.

*

Second Meeting with Sir Edmund Hillary

According to Sherpa statistics, we were supposed to have a snowfall in two days. The clouds grew menacing. The sun was completely hidden, and the air turned chilly when I met with Sir Edmund Hillary for the second time. Our two-hour conversation at the Hillary Hospital in the Sherpa village of Khunde was a happy one.

*

I had met this great man four years previously, while skiing in New Zealand. In Wellington, halfway up a hill, children were playing rugby on a grassy estate surrounded by forest. He was by the pool in the garden when I first saw him. I was surprised by his size; I had to crane my neck to see any part of him above the waist. The hand that I shook was huge. He laughed when I said that a person with such legs and arms must be able to climb with double the stride of an ordinary person.

His wife was lovely. When the children came home from school, he went down to the grass to join them—an unsophisticated man of the mountain—a real lover of nature.

Now, at our meeting in Nepal, Hillary spoke words which

I was finally getting in shape. *Photograph copyright © Akira Kotani.*

still remain in my heart. He said, "People must stay close to nature, especially little children. We must live in tune with the earth, draw strength and inspiration from her, and in return give her love and protection.

"Young people should wander through the forest, play in the lakes, climb mountains, and sail across the seas. Youth must try its strength against the uncompromising hand of nature.

"Only through testing and tempering can young people come to know who they are and what they are capable of doing. And only with that knowledge can they begin to cooperate with their friends and society at large."

Hillary had been helping the Sherpas build hospitals and schools, roads and bridges, with the support of the New Zealand lottery.

*

On the other hand, there was a Japanese businessman who was planning to buy the most scenic spot in the area and build a hotel on it. He was trying to borrow some money from the government of Nepal and build an airport to bring in tourists. I heard that he was having great difficulty because of strong opposition from the local residents. I don't think the idea of a hotel was completely wrong, but must they ruin the little fields of the Sherpas to build it? I wondered if the hotel, built at an elevation of thirteen thousand feet, would fit in with its surroundings. It was none of my business, and it is not polite to criticize somebody else's passion and work, but I really didn't wish to see Nepal become a tourist country. I hoped it would always remain the country of adventure, the country of expeditions.

*

Sir Edmund was amazed at my plan for skiing down Mount Everest. I had mentioned it to him half jokingly four years before at his house in Wellington. He had said it was impossible, and now it was coming true. He was very happy for me and shared lots of good advice and hard-won experience.

*

I learned that Norman Dyhrenfurth, captain of the U.S. Mount Everest expedition team, after hearing about our plan had commented that even if I were a superman, after spending one evening, one night, at a height of twenty-six thousand feet above sea level, I would find my energy level reduced tremendously, no matter how much oxygen I had. He thought it was impossible to ski at twenty-six thousand feet, where it was so strenuous just to walk.

*

Hillary said that violent activity at a height of twenty-six thousand feet could mean death, that I should conserve all my energies and power until the moment of starting, and that I should have as much team support as possible. There were quite a few world-class mountaineers who did not think kindly about this project of skiing down Mount Everest; I think they felt that the mountain belonged only to the mountaineers. They considered it a sacred place and didn't want others to be walking around their territory.

*

Our film producer, Mr. Zeniya, asked Hillary, as the world's first person to conquer Everest, what his opinion was of our project—also a world's first—to ski down the slope of Mount Everest. The quiet answer came back cheerfully: "People have stood face to face with difficult problems and moved forward as they pushed them aside. It will be the end when people lose heart and stop looking for new and challenging problems. If only I were younger and a little better skier myself, I would like to join you. For this reason I sincerely hope for your success."

*

The Difference Between Sherpas and Porters

One old Sherpa dropped out of the caravan and disappeared. Just like a candle, the flame of life was extinguished. His age was uncertain—probably a little over sixty. Nobody knew how he managed to get into our team. Ang Tsering, the *sirdar*, or head Sherpa, cocked his head. He said the old man was one of the Sherpas he had personally picked, but admitted that he was forced to take him by the Sherpas' Union, the Himalayan Society. Anyway, the old man himself had insisted that he was a high altitude Sherpa. He had said, "I am a Sherpa who has been to the South Col." We didn't know how he had done it, but he had managed to put the three lines on his hat indicating that he was a high altitude porter. All the low altitude porters who had only two lines on their hats were used to bring the loads to Base Camp where the high altitude Sherpas take over.

There are minor differences between the international expeditions that roam the Himalayas, but none of the larger expeditions make high altitude Sherpas carry luggage during the caravan; these Sherpas are treated the same as expedition personnel. They only carry their own personal things, like clothing and lunch. Low altitude porters, on the other hand, carry an average of seventy pounds. Even a child or old woman will carry up to about fifty pounds. The old porters were bending their backs in two, carrying seventy or eighty pounds. Not that we thought the Sherpas immortal, but it was unbelievable that a Sherpa who supposedly had been on expeditions going over twenty-six thousand feet would collapse on this present trek, which was sort of like a hike in the Japan Alps. A few days before people on the filming team had noticed his weakness. But when I found him lying in the trail, exhausted, and another time falling over coughing in the middle of a field, I decided to talk to the producer, Mr. Zeniya.

We felt that if something did go wrong, we would be sorry both for his sake and also for the expedition's. If he could get home at all, we should send him away. I guess what I meant was firing him. For a three-stripe Sherpa this might have been a worse fate than death. The doctor took him out of the team. Since we heard that his home was in Thyangboche, right on our route, we decided to relieve him of any work.

I was at the end of the line the day before we would reach the old Sherpa's home. I was walking in the forest along the river after having left the empty campsite at Phakdingma, when I ran into the old Sherpa, with messy hair and four days' worth of stringy beard. He was sitting on a rock, his arms dangling lifeless at his sides. His thin body looked even worse now that he was wearing new mountain-climbing shoes, knickers, and the red checkered shirt that had been supplied to him. I thought of giving him water, but I realized that little streams of water were running right beneath his feet. I asked him if he was all right, but there was no answer. I asked him whether he could walk. He shook his head vertically, which to a Sherpa means "no." I told him he would be all right and tomorrow he'd be home. "Take your time, take your time, take as long as you wish. You can dream about the twenty-six thousand-foot high road to Mount Everest." I took out a tube of honey from my backpack, added some vitamin pills and offered them to him with both hands. Then I hurried away and ran down the hill. He looked like a dead man.

*

After about twenty minutes of fast hiking I came to a one-log bridge, where I finally ran into three porters sitting around a campfire mixing up *tsamba* for breakfast. I washed my face, brushed my teeth, warmed up my frozen hands, and rested a little. I left the three people, saying, "*Namahste*," a Nepalese word meaning "hello," "good-by," and "I salute your eternal soul." I hurried toward the mountain pass, following a winding road through a darkening forest. I was striding along and suddenly, there he was—the old man that I had left. He could never have passed me. There was only one road. Besides, I had only rested a little by the bridge; how could he have gotten ahead of me? If the one that I had met before—the one that I had offered help with both hands—was alive, who could this be?

Later, in Thyangboche, I heard that the Sherpa had died on the trail. I felt like tearing out my hair in grief. I believed until the end of the caravan, until the end of the project, that one of them must have been a ghost.

*

Looking at Death

The head lama said: "That is the destiny of mankind. Everybody must face it some day. The fact that my father died and that he could not come back from Katmandu—that was destiny." We bowed our heads, and the chief lama of Thyangboche, who was called a living Buddha, closed his eyes with sorrow. The old Sherpa had been his father-in-law.

*

Phu Dorje's death had been a violent one, but this old Sherpa had encountered a very lonely, quiet death. He had just disappeared into the dark forest. I felt many times that our expedition was being followed by an unknown shadow. I really didn't want to think about it, but still, that ill feeling came to me once in a while in the dark of the night. I forced myself to act cheerfully, like a person doing calisthenics accompanied by the morning radio: "One, two, one, two. Let's be healthy today!"

*

At four-thirty I complained about the meals at camp. I asked, "What shall we eat to be able to work with confidence at twenty-six thousand feet?" What I meant was, with this kind of meal our bodies would disintegrate. Our dinner consisted of rice, a little vegetable soup, and some canned pickles. As a big eater, I was annoyed. The young people knew nothing about balanced nutrition. But I was too lazy to explain it to them. I knew we were going to be living together for a long time; I had to get into the habit of talking with a little more concern. "A little cushioning and padding goes a long way. It's a long strenuous trip. . . .

Let's not hurt people's feelings." That night I wrote a letter without thinking to whom I was going to mail it:

> I can see the stars from the tent. There is a song that says you can see stars and the moon from your window, but this is very much better. Last night the Sherpas had too much energy putting up the tent. They jammed the zipper so we could not close the entrance. Sleeping at the open flaps, I can see the stars. I can count them and talk to them while I am lying here.
>
> From the next tent I can hear the Sherpas' radio playing heavy Indian music as if stirring up a dark swamp. Even at a height of only seven thousand feet, the night is very cold. I wore my down parka at dinner. Anyway, since I am no longer talking to the stars, I must blow out my candle. Otherwise, they will be too shy to show their faces.

I could have just gone on and on writing these nonsense letters, so I decided to stop and sleep.

*

Abominable Snowman?

The Sherpas' prediction of snow was not quite right. The clouds kept floating by and did not stop to drop their loads. A Buddhist lama who had come to have dinner with us at our invitation, said it would snow the next day. Everybody was rather doubtful because there was that same blue sky with occasional clouds, but, sure enough, it started to snow the very next day. I thought I might be able to try skiing if it accumulated, but only four inches came down.

*

Our lama friend believed that the abominable snowman was real. We hoped to see one. We heard that the porters belonging to the expedition team of the Japanese Alpine Club, which had passed through here two weeks ago, ran away, saying that they had met a snowman while hiking through the mysterious forest by the river, a little below the temple. I brought up the subject with the porters and Sherpas while we were resting. They all started to talk at once. After the first sentence, which was something about so-and-so's cow dying of a broken neck, but not broken by a wolf or a mountain lion, the conversation became a wild shouting match in Sherpa. Even the translator got involved in the heated exchange. I couldn't understand any of it.

Most scientific opinion holds that the abominable snowman does not exist. The footprints that have been found are assumed to be those of other animals, their size having been exaggerated and distorted by the melting snow.

There are some authorities who do not quite agree with this formulation, and Norman Dyhrenfurth is one of them. He believes the yeti is one of a species of unknown anthropoids. Nobody has ever seen the animal, or at least there have been no reliable witnesses. Its existence depends on whether you believe in it or not. Some team members believed, and some did not. But everybody agreed that any animal would be terrified and flee if it found such a large and noisy expedition team marching toward it.

*

As usual, we somehow managed to organize the baggage, and arrived at our next camp completely exhausted. About ten o'clock that night we heard that two porters were missing, an old mute and a deaf mute. As I recalled, those two men looked rather unreliable. Five minutes after we had started, the old man had already collapsed once. We took half his load and divided it between Amma and myself, so we had extra-heavy packs to carry.

We were worried because the temperature would go down to zero at night, and those two did not even have their own blankets. What if they froze to death? They were carrying the parachutes and ski boots, since those were the lightest items available. We could not do without that equipment. We sent out the Sherpas to search for them with headlamps, carrying warm tea and food. The two couldn't be very far away. Some people had seen them halfway up the trail. They couldn't really have gotten lost either, because the night was clear and the visibility, good. But there were some loose rocks, and it seemed rather easy to fall into the moraine. There may have been a rockslide.

The Sherpas returned after searching for two hours, saying they could not find the two mutes. They were not very concerned because they believed one couldn't really die of exposure around here. "They are probably sleeping behind some rocks and will be back in the morning," they said.

*

I was awakened by some commotion outside the tent early the next morning. The porters had returned, and they claimed to have seen a snowman. "It had shiny eyes which spun in its head. We thought we were going to be eaten alive," gestured the mutes. They had huddled and trembled until the snowman had disappeared. After listening to the story, everyone started to laugh. I suppose those two had never seen electric headlamps. Especially since they were tired, confused by the thin air, cold and hungry, they could hardly be blamed for believing they had seen a snowman when they saw lights shining on distant heads and heard strange voices.

*

Abominable Mountaineers?

The Sherpas were jokingly saying that *bala sabu* (that's me!) must be a reincarnated abominable snowman. Perhaps three hundred years from now there will be a story told in the Sherpa villages of a snowman who sped at tremendous speed down the side of Chomolungma, which some foreigners call Mount Everest. He was a small snowman named Miura, and he was of the *choti* type of snowman, which causes nobody any trouble, though by all accounts his conduct was strange. The story would be passed from mouth to mouth by the old Sherpas.

*

My own theories on the snowman are simple. There was once a sneaky bandit who blamed his burglary and cattle rustling on the yeti. Or else the whole thing is an overblown children's story. In the snow country where I was born, we were told to go to bed early on snowy nights because the "snowwoman" might come and snatch us. I remember being very scared. Maybe the story of the snowwoman became that of the yeti in the Himalayas.

Our group was not interested in searching for the snowman. We were considered almost snowmen ourselves. We were certainly drunken, abominable mountaineers. And we had to be careful that the Sherpas didn't run away from us.

*

Mountains and Sea
It is unwise to repeat the same tactic several times. If you fail once with an attack, there is little chance for success if you try a second time. If you fail twice, you must change your method of attack or suffer certain defeat.
If the enemy thinks of the mountains, attack like the sea. If he thinks of the sea, attack like the mountains.

MUSASHI "Ring of Fire"

*

Eat and Sleep

Weather clear. A day of resting, just doing nothing all day long. I was awakened at six o'clock in the morning by an irate monk. I had managed to sneak into a school for Buddhist lamas in order to sleep. I had planned to sleep late in their dining room, but they woke me up and chased me out.

It was glorious weather. There were some peculiar clouds yesterday, but they cleared away during the night. I had really liked the weather lately; it was consistent. It always stayed clear till noon; in the afternoons, the sky was covered with tired-looking clouds, and everything became very pale. We were pretty close to heaven, but still not quite there.

*

Our troop left for Mingbo Glacier to get adjusted to the altitude. In the morning I managed to join the group that was supposed to leave early. I ate breakfast at six-thirty, raring to go, but at eight-thirty I ate another breakfast while the group still rested. I think I ate too much. We never did get started that day.

I leisurely took the things out of my backpack to air them, and after I had asked a Sherpani to do my laundry I lay down on my air mattress and fell asleep. I had read the travelogue of Tibet by Eikai Kawaguchi. At the end of the book he said that even a dedicated hermit like himself had not discovered the secrets of the universe during his wanderings in the Himalayas. He was ashamed of himself, but he made up his mind to go back to Japan, realizing that if he tried as hard in Japan, he wouldn't learn any less than he had in the Himalayas.

It was very quiet. I felt as if my soul and body were going to melt into the mountain. My only complaint was a light case of diarrhea. But even that was not too bad, since it forced me to stop frequently and admire the grand scenery.

*

At breakfast I tried to scare people by saying that if their beards grew too long, they would collect icicles and get frostbite on their faces. To my surprise, cameraman Kanau and all the others admitted that they were thinking of shaving off their beards but needed some excuse. "Today's a good day, let's go and shave, let's go and shave," they all said. We all went down to a nearby stream together for a shaving party.

*

In the evening, just as I was getting ready to start my training, Dr. Motoyama caught me to use as a guinea pig for the electrocardiograph. I did my ski training plugged into a machine. After about an hour of this encumbered exercise, I joined the Sherpas for a game of badminton. It was a little strange. Although there was no wind, the shuttlecock kept sailing out of bounds. I realized it was because of the thin air.

*

In Japan, people say that the best way to digest properly is to fill your stomach only 80 percent full. "At high altitudes," Tonko says, "it is best to fill up only 70 percent." (In Tonko's case, he would fill up the rest of his stomach with sake!) My hard-won advice for mountaineers is that you shouldn't eat too much, and you shouldn't eat too much strange food, like yak meat. Also, you shouldn't launch into any strenuous activity right after you have eaten. Rest first. Keep your stomach warm, even while exercising. You should rub yourself with dry cloths every morning in order to help your circulation. Be sure also to get some light exercise before breakfast.

*

Mr. Matsukata Hardly Looks Seventy Years Old

We were in the Solo Khumbu region, the heart of Sherpa country. At thirteen thousand feet above sea level, in a sacred meadow with a fine view of Mount Everest, we stayed for five days in order for the team members to get adjusted to the altitude. I wrote a letter to a friend, but never mailed it. Unmailed letters make up some of my best journal notes.

Dear Nobuko,

How many days have gone by or how many years have gone by? Even though it is March, it feels like February; floating through the day, I have forgotten time. I can see Everest right in front of my eyes, right in front of the tent where I am writing this letter. This is noon of the fifth day we have spent at this sacred meadow by a Buddhist temple in Thyangboche. The caravan decided to rest at this point, so I took a nap and slept like a log in the mud.

I went to attend a lunch-time tea party at the head lama's chambers. The head lama is the highest ranking monk in this area. He is called a living Buddha. They offered us tea and *chapati,* the Tibetan pancake, with a prayer for the success and safety of the ski trip.

The head of the Japanese Alpine Club also arrived here,

yesterday afternoon. He was so energetic you could hardly believe he was seventy years old. Meeting Mr. Matsukata impressed me deeply. Isn't it wonderful for a man of his age to stroll happily through the Himalayas? Thirty-three years more for me! I don't know whether it is a long time or a short time.

The tea party at the head lama's was held in a little guest room next to the prayer hall. Our team members asked many questions, especially about the difference between Tibetan and Japanese Buddhism. I asked three questions. What do you, as the head lama, think of yeti? What does the word *Chomolungma* mean, and are there any old myths about it? When Sherpas—or any Nepalese—pass a religious tower, they always pass on the left. Why is that? Or if they do manage to pass on the wrong side, will they be punished for it, and if so, by what kind of punishment?

Those were three rather useless questions, but the answers I received were interesting: concerning the yeti, the people of Tibet and the Sherpas believe in their existence. There are two kinds of yeti: one of them is called *choti*, a very small and quiet creature, and the other is called *miti*, a violent, monstrous snowman. The head lama himself said he had seen one while standing at the door of the temple a few years ago. I have heard that porters passing through the forest have run away thinking that they had seen a snowman, but it seems that the yeti do not like civilized people, including myself, since they have never appeared in front of us during our expedition.

Chomolungma, the Tibetan name for Mount Everest, means the "mother goddess riding on a tiger." The tiger is the long mountain chain of surrounding peaks.

Concerning the rule that pedestrians should walk on the left side of *chortens*, the people of Nepal believe that God and the king exist only on the right-hand side and should be kept there. The officer who acted as my interpreter got so involved in the conversation that he failed to relay all the answers, but we all spent a very delightful time. Three of us, Taisuke, Don-chan, and I, were invited to visit the head lama's room for some sacred medicine and a chant.

The march is due to start again tomorrow morning, leaving ten people behind in poor condition. We set April 29 as the day for the downhill.

If everything goes well, the dream will come true on that day, but I am not rushing; I am just going to let it happen.

*

There Are Three Methods for Taking the Lead:

The First

Attack first, calmly and quickly. Or you can advance strongly but with obvious reserve, catch your opponent off-guard as he tries to understand the reasons for your reserve.

Or advance with as deliberate and strong a spirit as possible. When you reach the enemy and have judged his committed response to your rhythm of attack, quicken your pace and sharply overwhelm him.

Or, with a calm and concentrated spirit, attack with the feeling of totally crushing the enemy, from first to last. Your spirit should conquer him to the depths.

The Second

When the enemy attacks, let your spirit remain undisturbed but feign weakness. When the enemy reaches you, move away, indicating your intent to leap aside. Then, as soon as you see him relax, drive home your strongest attack.

Or, when your enemy attacks, reply with a fiercer attack, taking advantage of the resultant break in his timing to triumph.

The Third

When the enemy makes a strong attack, reply with calm and poise, seek out the weak points in his strategy, and use them to win.

Or, if the enemy attacks calmly, harmonize with his movements with your body floating, then move quickly and cut him with strength.

The principles of strategy are conveyed in terms of single combat, but you must think broadly; the principles are equally applicable for ten-thousand-a-side battles and the lonely, internal struggle for wisdom.

MUSASHI "Ring of Fire"

*

Heavier Load

"A man who is to receive glory must bear a heavier burden of responsibility than others." I was inclined to believe this ancient Shinto aphorism. Up to this point, I had headed along the road of glory with a heavy load of luggage on my back. I had breezed along with the caravan at great speed, always increasing the weight of my burden. Ever since we passed Namche, that tension has eased a little. It was necessary to relax. Since we have been in the mountains, everything has been uphill. I have enjoyed it. The downhill decay of the spirit is more painful than uphill climbing with the body.

In thirty days or so, I must become a man appropriate for the pages of the history of the world's adventures. I must take the necessary steps to be both able and worthy of the risk. I must endure the suffering of increased training that I may even hope for victory.

*

Eleven at night. Outside the tent, I could see the Sherpas on watch, patrolling with their lights. The almost full moon washed away all the colors and polished the ice and rocks of the mountains into carved silver.

At night we could hear the silence of the world, tolling across the mountains of our imaginations. Standing in this glorious silence, how wonderful the earth felt.

I kept wondering, "Is it really all right to be standing like this, so free and so peaceful? Haven't I forgotten something important? Shouldn't I be worried and frustrated, like my friends back in Tokyo?" I decided to climb the next day with a heavier weight on my back.

*

The Road to Lobuje

The five days of rest weren't so healthful. I slept too much, ate too much, and drank too much, which made me even more tired. The diarrhea made me less energetic. I started the day without breakfast. "*Bistali, bistali.*" I planned to slow down in two weeks at the Everest Base camp for about a week, in order not to overburden my heart. Then I could gradually increase my pace all the way until April

29, when my strength would peak for the great ski descent. I was careful not to overdo my conditioning program. "If I attempt too much and crack up, I can never recover my strength in time," I told myself. I decided to conserve my energy for later needs.

*

Passing by the foot of Ama Dablam on the way to Pheriche, I stopped to shave with an electric razor. Two gentle old Sherpa men came by and stopped in amazement. They peered very closely, almost touching my face, and watched me shave with great delight. I washed my underwear in the beautiful creek past the house of Jambu, the kitchen boy. The water was cold enough to paralyze my hands, so I tried it Nepalese style, putting the soap on the clothes and then slapping them on the rocks. That wasn't too bad. I leaned against a warm rock after a little climb and read Tensing's record of the first successful Mount Everest expedition.

*

I began eating less in order to flatten my stomach, but my energy level decreased. You can't lose weight in a hurry. It takes time.

A Sherpani passed by with two loaded yaks. I walked along with some kitchen boys and stopped for lunch with them. Taisuke noted that the Sherpas ate honey while we ate canned tangerines, and canned pineapple when we ate canned peaches. I agreed that the food on this expedition left much to be desired; as proof, most of the young team members had trouble recovering from the many diseases which attacked them. The ignorance of Japanese people about their bodies appalled me. It was not the money, but why did we have to spend tens of thousands of dollars buying those awful instant foods and canned junk? I guess it was partly our fault; we put the young team members completely in charge of the food and they knew nothing about nutrition.

*

Profession

Three days later, there was some snow in Lobuje. We had changed our plans, and four of us—my skiing disciple, Tak, cameraman Kotani, a reporter, and I—decided to stay for a while and enjoy it. I put on my skis for a workout at fourteen thousand feet and felt no strain. Walking every day had done some good!

I received a letter by runner from our scouts at the Everest Base Camp that evening:

> Dear Mr. Miura:
>
> According to information from the Japanese Alpine Club, the condition of the icefall is very bad, and the Bergschrund in the center is getting worse. From the Base Camp, the mountains surrounding the area seem to have only half the amount of snow compared to last fall, and the area around the icefall and the Base Camp now has shiny ice in many spots. Looking from Gorakshep, there is very little snow, and the upper course is completely cut off. Sorry we can't be more accurate, but this is all we have to report.
>
> PS to Mr. Kotani: the Base Camp is wonderfully equipped."

It looked like we were going to have more trouble than any of us had imagined.

*

I had dinner with a Japanese party on their way back from Everest Base Camp. They confirmed the report that the South Col was unusually bare and rocky, and also that the south wall of Mount Everest was very exposed and icy this year. With conditions so bad, it would be no disgrace if we could not climb to the South Col. I was a little nervous, so I said that even if it were shameful to quit, we shouldn't be afraid to use the word. Glossing over a disgrace would only throw away our courage to try again.

*

The next morning Taisuke asked me, "What is a professional skier?" My answer was rather vague, since I was still asleep. "Being a professional is a state of mind. You can't really feed yourself all year long just because you're a good skier. If you are an instructor, you are limited by the seasons. And there's not much money in being a professional racer either, unless you are one of the best. My favorite part is teaching others something they can enjoy in the outdoors."

That night at dinner, I held forth on the world of professional skiing. "There is no difference in the technique, the discipline, or the effort that professionals and amateurs put in; they always do their best. But amateurs have to follow the rules made by other people. For instance, first-class amateurs only gain glory when they put everything they have into competing in the Olympics or the World Cup Championships. They live in competition day and night, and their success is their sole return. Professional skiers experience the same thing, and there are many professional skiers who compete in those games and win medals. But for professionals, there is something more. By putting your entire self into skiing, not only in competition with other people but with yourself, too, you can touch people's hearts with creativity. Professionals can dedicate themselves completely to mastering the highest techniques. A professional instructor has the possibility of uncovering the beauty and goodness in other human beings by sharing the joys of movement."

My philosophy consists of seeking a new dimension of excellence, beyond professionalism and amateurism. They are only terms of convenience which people have set up arbitrarily.

The things we must develop are sincerity in one's self, joyous effort, and a willingness to explore all possibilities. Increasing numbers of people with such qualities will help human beings learn to trust each other, and to unfold their wings of imagination and hope, like young birds leaving the nests of the past. To professionals, categorizing between professionals and amateurs is unnecessary; being a professional allows one to grow and develop through one's work as long as one lives. I have told myself, "This is how I want to live," and I do.

*

Training at Sixteen Thousand Feet

I found Tadano skiing in some leftover snow around the tent. I decided to nap, since I didn't really feel like skiing; I was too tired after walking all day, and the snowy patches between the rocks were ridiculously narrow.

*

3:30 P.M. I woke up, and since I was wasting time just sleeping, I decided to join the skiing. Terrible snow! The surface had started to freeze while the ground was still warm: the four inches of snow was like coarse sugar. Our skis scraped on the rocks. When the sun went down, the snow finally started to freeze through, and the skiing got easier. I was rusty at first and felt that I might slip at any time and crash into the rocks. But after making a series of small, continuous turns, I regained my confidence. The familiar, vibrant feeling of boots, skis, and snow tickled the soles of my feet.

The snow and the slopes were nowhere near perfect, but they were the best we had, and therefore quickly became enjoyable. I did not tire. We were skiing at 16,000 feet—higher than the peak of Mont Blanc. It was only natural that we ran out of breath, but I was pleased with the speed of my recovery. I skied about two hours, ignoring the dinner call As I skied, I regretted having to leave this place so soon. Once we left here, we wouldn't be able to ski until we reached 18,500 feet, above the icefall and the Base Camp. I discussed it with Don-chan and decided to remain a few more days for ski training. At dusk cameraman Kotani came to visit. We talked late into the night.

*

To Know the Times
    Know the enemy's disposition in battle. Is it confident or
uncertain? By observing the spirit of the enemy's men you can choose
appropriately advantageous positions.
    Knowing the times means seeing through events to the spirit and
strategy within. If you are well enough versed in the patterns of
strategy, you will recognize your enemy's intentions and find many
opportunities to win.
                                        MUSASHI "Ring of Fire"

*

Sexy Mountains and Ancient Wisdom

Everybody had gone except for Kotani, Tadano, a
reporter, me, and three Sherpas. Only two tents were left.
We didn't do much; we skied a little, and the rest of the
time just lay around. Sometime after lunch Kotani asked me,
"What do you think about the triangle shape on Nuptse?" In
the center of Nuptse, which juts into the sky out of the
Khumbu glacier, it looks like a black triangle. We came up
with some dirty jokes. I don't know how to explain the
sensuous feeling that oozed out of that mountain, but it was
certainly there—that part of the mountain looked very sexy.
Its delicate, curved lines disappeared mysteriously into the
glacier. We never got tired of looking at it and stared at it
for hours.

*

I decided to climb a nearby rocky peak and reached the
top within an hour. The air wasn't too clear from where I
was, but I peered down at the Base Camp and the icefall at
the foot of Everest. I just sat staring at the world of rock, ice,
and sky. "The scenery looks like mortgaged property on
the moon," I thought in commercial Japanese fashion.

*

That night I had a very sincere and profound
conversation with cameraman Kotani. He was in a rare
mood. His words had depth, like the lost sayings of our
ancestors. He was striving to put into words the spirit of our
traditional culture.

I think among modern people the ancient wisdom has

almost disappeared; we are only left with the repetition of injunctions from our parents: do this, don't do that. The experience the ancients gained by wandering over the earth is lost today because the way of life is lost; it is almost impossible to find such wisdom among men. In the few words from the past that have been found after much seeking, people have rediscovered the spirit that encourages action, steels the mind, clarifies dreams, and awakens the questions, laughter, and anger of life. It has always been difficult to find a person with such a magical power of language. If you can find a friend with that power, listen well.

*

To Renew
    When in the heat of conflict you are deadlocked with your opponent with no possible resolution, rethink the situation with a fresh spirit, and establish a new rhythm.
    "To renew" means without changing your physical position, you change your spirit, perceive new opportunities, and triumph.

MUSASHI "Ring of Fire"

*

Renewal

I decided to make this short stay at Lobuje with these few people something precious. This was a time to think about the future and tend the little garden in which the spirit can fly free. I felt that in this place of natural beauty, in this silent time, I could purify my mind and body and restore my energy.

I think that people need to keep their numbers in balance. The bigger the crowd, the more violent its power. Too often, it crushes people. Crowding generates a great wind that blows sand and dust into people's hearts.

I enjoyed the caravan very much, but there were too many people in it. I wanted to be alone, yet I was depressingly alone in that great, unfeeling crowd walking along the dusty trails.

*

At night there were stars stuck in the sky, and just before the moon came out, I was reminded of a small skiing place in the Japanese countryside, nestled amid mountains and snow-covered forest. Although I was surrounded by rocks and monstrous, icy mountains, I felt some nostalgia for the small beauties at home.

Morning. The day had broken without any sound—peaceful—everything in the world was peaceful. I mumbled gratefully as I ate my breakfast, "Even the crows in Tibet are peaceful." They must have heard me; one gave two loud cries and gave me a dirty look, as if to say, "What do you think I am, a hummingbird?" and flew away.

I took a closer look at the black birds that flew in packs. They had yellow beaks and were a little smaller than the crows at home. I asked a Sherpa, and he told me that those birds were called *kakakuri*. They flew up to heights of twenty-three thousand feet around the glacier. They were very happy, gentle birds, the Sherpa said, and they never drank water out of a puddle, only rain water. How refined! Though now they had the shapes of birds, originally they were true lovers who died knowing that they could never be together in this world. As I watched, though they seemed to be flying in groups, they were really couples. Slowly, they disappeared into the sky in pairs.

Our expedition zoologist said later that they were a species of mynah bird. But the crow that I had heard was a Tibetan crow called a *gorak* by the natives. He looked like a gangster and flew off as if air were leaking through his wings. When I first saw the black birds, I thought they were black eagles. They appeared to have a nine-foot wingspread.

The real Himalayan eagles, however, are truly monstrous—so big they can pick up a sheep. Some Nepalese and Tibetans believe that if birds eat the flesh of people after they have died, their spirits go to heaven. One great eagle landed on a rock near the tent. Cameraman Kotani came out hurriedly to take some photographs. The eagle seemed to be purposely posing, looking stern and proud, a carrier of departed souls.

One further bird that catches the eye is the *ptarmigan*. They nest among the rocky peaks, but when people come close, they run away like the airplanes of Nepal—very unsteadily, like a fat cow taking off. One ungainly member of our filming crew was called Mr. Ptarmigan.

*

We were completely taken by surprise when a long-haired, bearded American crawled out from behind a great rock about a hundred yards above our tent. Nepal, especially Katmandu, was known as the hippie paradise of the world in 1969. I was astonished once while swimming in a pool in a suburb of Katmandu, when a young American woman burst out of the bushes, took off her clothes, and dove into the pool.

We were happy to meet anyone and politely invited the young man to join us for breakfast. He was in the U.S. Peace Corps. Despite his looks, he didn't seem very much different from anyone else. He was a very happy and cheerful young man, good-natured but conservative. He said he had been living in the Terai area of Nepal for the past three years, teaching agricultural techniques. He was taking a vacation with two brothers and some friends from California in order to see Mount Everest. He said he felt rather lost in this cold climate, having come from tropical Terai onto an icy glacier. The day before, he had gone to Everest Base Camp with two others, and this morning, those two had gone to climb Kala Pattar, but he himself had a headache probably from too much excitement yesterday—and had decided to stay behind and get some sun. Lazy people get to know lazy people, and we became friends.

*

Over a breakfast of *chapati* and black tea he told us a funny story about the people of Nepal. The far inland region of Terai is a jungle, not unlike that of India, but swarming with elephants and tigers. "The people can't understand that the earth is round," he said. He had spent days and days trying to explain and had even asked his friends to send him a map of the world and a globe. Do you know what the natives said in the end? "Yeah, sure, but where is this America in India?" So he tried to explain again that the earth is round, just like the moon, and that Nepal was on one side while America was on the other side. The Nepalese called him a liar when he gave a long explanation of how *Apollo 11* was launched to the moon. They said, "If the United States is down below us, how come the rocket went straight up toward the moon, which is above us? Therefore the earth must be flat, just as the Hindu Gods always say. Besides, since we let you talk, you keep saying that Nepal is a very small country, but do you know how many days it takes us to reach Katmandu? How can you say it's such a small country when it takes more than a month of walking to get there?" Since then they don't trust the Peace Corps very much.

"With accuracy only, you can never reach the truth." Are these words of Hegel true? Even for us, the top of Mount Everest, which was only ten kilometers away as the crow flies, seemed as distant as the moon.

*

To Become the Enemy

Think yourself into the enemy's position and discover his fears and weaknesses. People tend to think of an enemy trapped inside a house as a strongly fortified opponent. However, if we use the strategy "To Become the Enemy," we realize that for the one who is trapped the world stands against us, and there is no escape. He who is trapped inside, no matter how strong his fortifications, is a pheasant. He who enters to arrest is a hawk.

In single combat you must put yourself in the enemy's position. If he is thinking, "Here is a master of the Way, who knows the principles of strategy," you will surely defeat him. If, however, he thinks himself superior, use the Three Methods for Taking the Lead. [See p. 94.]

MUSASHI "Ring of Fire"

*

A Private Trip

Breakfast: Curry. I didn't really have an appetite, so I only ate some soup and *tsamba*. My diarrhea finally stopped. I had scraped my left leg on some rocks and didn't feel like skiing. "I'll have to take it easy, now. I must be in perfect health when I begin ski training above the icefall in a few days." Without physical activity, I was bored, completely bored.

An athlete's body has an intellectual and artistic life of its own. It speaks a language of rhythm in phrases of effort, technique, and alternating stress and relaxation. Like a musical instrument properly played, the body soars between exhilaration and pathos, riding the winds of adrenaline's urges.

The mind can know the world only by deduction, sorting out the incoming streams of sensory, verbal and contemplative information into some rational and, inevitably, illusory whole. But the body is physical substance in a world of the same. And an athlete's body, integrating both artist and medium, expresses itself in form and motion.

Through training I had struggled to awaken my body's power, and succeeded. Now, I had to contend with this forceful almost separate intelligence, which, deprived of its daily self-expression, fought back with anger, anxiety and apathy.

*

Tak had taken off his clothes and was getting some sun. Cameraman Kotani was writing a letter. Some members of the team were stretched out in their tents with headaches, while a group of Sherpas was kicking a soccer ball around a terraced field. I took an air mattress outside the tent, put a sleeping bag on top of it, and lay down to read a book by Norman Dyhrenfurth on Nepal. I fell asleep under the high Himalayan sun.

*

One morning, I was snacking on Sherpa-style curried potatoes when I got the urge to take a trip. Watching the clouds drift over the peaks, I felt like drifting too. It seemed rather strange to want to take a trip after having come all the way here to Everest. But for the last three weeks traveling with the caravan had seemed as mechanical as the excursion trips we took in grade school. We began walking at sunrise on the appointed road, reached the next campsite in the afternoon, and gathered around when called for dinner. We lived amid the noise of eight hundred people from morning till night. It was a happy experience in its own way. But I felt richer and more peaceful with this little party here at Lobuje.

*

The name of the mountain was Pokalde; it was about eighteen thousand feet high. I did not really have to make many preparations to strike out on my little trip. Sunshine filtered through my half-closed eyes. I could see a small mountain glacier whose slopes shone and glistened in the light. I put on my down-filled suit, packed a change of clothes, potatoes, brown sugar, *chapati*, black tea, and my attaché case filled with all my notes and books into my backpack, put on my mountain boots, and left. I turned into an ant, jumping over the unsteady rocks of this giant anthill for half an hour. Climbing over the last huge moraine, thinking I had made it to the top, I spied a great gorge about a thousand feet below, with the real summit up the other side. I ran down and then climbed a grassy forty-degree incline that continued up another thousand yards. I went softly so as not to get out of breath, as if I were climbing an icefall. It turned into rock climbing at the halfway point. By good guessing I found a natural route and went for it, blindly thinking that I might be the first one on top. It was a long afternoon of slow climbing, clinging onto rocks, and kicking steps in the ice. I wished I had brought my crampons. I finally reached the top, with the thought occasionally flashing in my mind that if I fell, that would be the end of everything. There was already a cairn on top of the mountain. I decided to add a few more rocks to the cairn to honor my friends, both alive and dead.

*

The Meaning of Life

Let's walk the earth. To walk, I think, is the most wonderful exercise for human beings. When I return to Japan, I am going to walk around Kamakura, Mount Fuji, the Japan Alps, and the mountains of Hakoda. With my children I will walk. I will walk forever.

It is good to run, but to walk slowly and steadily, to walk all day, to walk from morning till sundown is the greatest joy. If you run, you can't stop to hang from the trees or climb on rocks or try push-ups or gymnastics; all those things that you want to do or have to do, you won't do if you run. Let's walk instead, over the mountains, along the seashore, let's walk.

*

Rock climbing at Lobuje. Tighten up my boots. I put my hands on the wall and climb. I am still a little tired from yesterday and have a headache, and there's this overhang looming dark and deadly above.

Lift my body in the air and let the rock take care of me—a little moment of tension—slip myself into the cracks between the rocks and the sky—look for the route overhead—I reached the top and enjoyed the view all the more for having worked hard to get there.

When it's cloudy, the air at sixteen thousand feet is full of an evil wind which turns the world to ice. Fog clings like a mourning shroud to the rocky peaks that surround the glacier. I did some hard exercising for an hour on top of the rocky face.

*

Let's not grieve about the present. In ancient times the Gods invited the moon, the stars, and the sun to accompany them in singing and living. But now they have all gone home.

*

Free and happy people once wandered the wilderness amid the rustling of the wind. Their sad descendants, wet and trembling, are the people of today.

*

If we lose the bright sunshine and the gentle breeze, our hearts will catch an eternal cold. Now is the time to bring back the sun, and call back the moon and the stars to be our friends.

*

"Open up the world for us to understand!" I cried in my heart to the snow covered peaks and the sky. "We are alive now, at this moment. We are alive!" My body went rigid as my spirit spread, swooping in all directions, filling and embracing the world. After a while my exhilaration passed and I started to lament the return of mundane consciousness. I told myself, "If now is everything let's not grieve about it. The future's only certainty is getting old—it's unpredictable and tortuous, like promises the rich may make when they are in a good mood."

*

Phu Dorje

Gorakshep—"the Crow's Cemetery." As the name indicates, it was a very lonely place. A cold wind blew northward carrying a mixture of dust and a little snow—I stood by the sandy pond where Phu Dorje and I dove and swam last year. Phu Dorje had pointed to the water and said, "By the time we return, this little lake will be frozen." But in the fall Phu Dorje had become a person of no return; he had gone to rest in the icy tomb of Everest, and as he had told me, the little lake, which we passed on our way back from the scouting trip, had started to freeze. It was completely frozen now. If he were alive, he would probably say, "*Bala sabu,* by the time we come back, this little lake will be filled with blue water."

*

Confusion at Base Camp

We marched toward Everest, a world of sky, rock, and ice, where only people with a hot desire to live could survive. In the evening I climbed Kala Pattar, the black rocky mountain near Gorakshep. I was moving strongly and easily, and before I knew it, I had already come to the top. Looming above the expedition Base Camp I could see the Khumbu icefall, looking as if it were splashing between Everest and Lhotse. Because it was cloudy, I doubted that I could see the top of Everest. But it slowly materialized through the fog. I could see the South Col and the slope where I hoped to ski. In between the black south walls of Everest and Lhotse, I could see the Col's whiteness shining in the sunset. As the sky grew dark, at the foot of the Khumbu glacier the lights of Base Camp began to glitter. It looked like an unfinished Disneyland on the moon.

*

Don-chan was distributing mountain-climbing boots, ice axes, and crampons to the Sherpas. The "Everest Restaurant," the shelter Tonko had built, was enormous. It was only yellow plastic sheets on top of piled rock walls, but already there were tables and chairs, shelves of books, and magazines inside, and a videotape player with enough prerecorded programs to keep us entertained for a month.

*

The glaciers were wild and cruel. The icefall looked as though a giant hammer had smashed whole mountains of ice and left the rubble behind.

The great chunks of ice were called *seracs,* and people who walked among them looked smaller than fleas. Each *serac* was the size of a small house.

Amid this glowering world of ice and rocks, our tent

Fat Taisuke sweats off some pounds at Everest Base Camp.

Photograph copyright © Kazunari Yasuhisa.

village was a bubble of happy feelings. It filled up the area with excitement and noise, so welcome when lonely, so obtrusive when not.

*

Tonko was in charge of Base Camp. He was a real magician. He could fix anything, jury-rig any mechanical or electrical device. What's more, he knew where every piece of equipment, clothing, or junk was stashed throughout the camp. If you asked for it, he might even present you with just one sock. Things were packed and repacked over and over again, and from this confusion order emerged.

*

Preparations for the final performance proceeded. The basic plan was, rush everything. The later the season, the more difficult the climbing, the thinner the skiing. We had heard that the monsoon would come early this year, but we still had to haul all our equipment up ten thousand feet: skis, cameras, tents and food, parachutes and oxygen tanks, and all the general mountain-climbing equipment. Furthermore, we had to get those cameramen and skiers who had never climbed mountains all the way up to the South Col. I don't imagine there was ever a Himalayan expedition that carried so much luggage.

Come to think of it, all we had done so far was to walk from Katmandu. Nothing had really begun. *Everything starts right now.* The long trek had acclimated us to the height and conditioned our muscles and lungs. At an altitude of seventeen thousand feet, we were so comfortable it felt as if we were lounging on a beach—when we weren't doing anything.

But it was hard work once we started moving around. I spent all day preparing my skis. Before dinner, I exercised on the ski machine. I did much better than I had imagined—a hundred jumps, another hundred, and then another, paying special attention to breathing stronger and faster. When tired, I counted the number of breaths instead of jumps. I performed much better at seventeen thousand feet than when I was in bad condition in Katmandu. Fifty push-ups; I did them continuously, and my arms started to tremble from cold and lack of oxygen.

*

Hard exercise stimulates the spirit and nourishes the mind. Though I was physically tired during the trek, there was always a song in my head. Stopping my body here at Base Camp seemed to have stopped my mind, too.

I guessed the thing to do was to keep moving. I decided to go skiing and headed off toward the icefall with my skis, but the surface was shiny blue ice. The pole tips glanced off like glass. After Tadano narrowly missed breaking his leg in a crevasse, we quickly returned to camp.

*

Tragedy at the Icefall

Thinking that we would have nothing to do until the support group set up camp at the base of Lhotse, we decided to go skiing at a glacier called Shangri-La, a day's walk from Gorakshep, and about two days from Base Camp. Eighteen or nineteen thousand feet wasn't too high for rigorous skiing, and it didn't look dangerous. At any rate, the ski team had nothing to do while the support team negotiated the icefall, carrying luggage to establish a high camp. And it didn't make sense for the skiers to go to the icefall just to get used to the altitude, since it was such a dangerous spot. So we went to Shangri-La. The filming team came along too.

*

As we were sorting gear inside our tents, preparing to leave, the tragedy happened. There was a loud commotion outside. Somebody shouted, "Something horrible in the icefall!" Kotani peered worriedly through the telescope. "I hope there hasn't been an accident." But he knew there had been. We had all gotten used to the bellow and roar of avalanches. There were big ones almost every day. Ishihara Productions was filming at the place where the avalanche started and thus probably recorded one of the world's largest avalanches. None of the camera team was hurt in that tidal wave of snow, and we were praying optimistically, when a series of loud reports crackled over the transceiver.

*

On this day almost all the members of the support team, with about thirty Sherpas, were in action, moving through the icefall at the same time. The Japanese Alpine Club had passed over the same course with an equal-sized party shortly before. We had hoped to start at five o'clock in the morning, but since this route was being opened by the Alpine Club, it would have been rude to start earlier than they. Since they had decided to start at six o'clock, we set our starting time for seven. A seven o'clock start on the most dangerous zone of the mountain seemed a little late, but the experts on glaciers said that icefalls move all the time. Since they never stop moving, there's no time safer than another. There was always the possibility that somebody would be killed. An early start made no difference. "It all depends on luck," they said. I supposed that was partly true.

*

At first, we were unable to find out who had been involved in the accident; the icefall was still very unstable. We could not tell when it might start again. The only thing we were able to do was to make sure of the identity of those who were unhurt and look for those who had disappeared into the crevasses. When we heard the voice over the radio say, "Two bodies have been identified," we hoped there would be no more, but that prayer, too, was useless. The number of casualties climbed, and still there were people missing. We had no way of finding out who they were.

Somebody was crying outside the tent. It was the child of the Sherpa Mimma Norbu, who was nicknamed "Little

Elephant." His father had gone up with the luggage. He sensed the death of his father even before the names of the dead were known.

*

The icefall remained unstable. More could crumble at any moment. Don-chan decided to move the bodies out of the accident area. Last year we were unable to do anything after Phu Dorje's accident; Ishiguro went a hundred feet into the crevasse to look for the bodies, but found that it was impossible to get them out unless we used dynamite to break up a block of ice as big as a building that stood in our way.

This year, there were lots of witnesses, and the victims were quickly discovered. Six Sherpas had died. I felt helpless, like a boat sinking in an empty ocean. I could feel the energy draining out of my body, and I was suddenly very tired. Who could explain this unfairness? Even the death of one person had caused a great empty hole, but six was too much. The great icefall took away six lives just on a whim. Everyone has to die someday, but why now? Why did it have to happen at this moment?

It requires a great amount of effort to survive here, but why did the innocent Sherpas have to die? Did they have to die because of their loyalty? How could the others recover and go back to work after seeing their comrades swallowed? How could they walk into the same trap, which might lead them, too, into the violent world of death?

*

Mount Everest Gets Further Away

Weather clear. I dreamed last night that I went to school with my children. I wonder if it's because my mind was so tired. I felt very far away from that happy domestic life with my children, and it was getting further away every day.

Mount Everest, which had appeared to come closer, had suddenly disappeared into the distance. With all the team

Paper fish are good luck. This expedition needed some.

Photo copyright © Akira Kotani.

Ready for takeoff. *Photo copyright © Akira Kotani.*

Funeral services for the Sherpas. *Photo copyright © Akira Kotani.*

The caravan marches relentlessly toward Everest. *Photo copyright © Akira Kotani.*

Ski fun. *Photo copyright © Akira Kotani.* ▶

The ski expedition is finished. We raise our flag and return to friends below.

Photo copyright © Akira Kotani.

members and Sherpas participating, we completed transporting the dead bodies by evening.

*

The end of the sad ceremony. Everybody dies sometime, but this was too early. The end came even before it had begun. Because it had happened in so cruel a manner, instead of giving a prayer to God, I was filled with anger. Watching the wives and children of the victims crying out in their grief, I was gripped by the hopelessness and emptiness of human life. But to submit myself to that darkness would only be an escape.

We must believe that after we shed our tears there must be something, some force which can help us overcome the onslaught of death. We must pray to that force, or we will never see the light of life again. Sorrow comes to us like waves carrying us out to sea, but if we are alive, we must be able to surface from whatever depths we sink and breathe in life again. "This may apply to me someday," I thought.

Grief at times seems cruel, but while we live we must value and accept it. As for anger against sudden death, we must keep the spark of life burning in order to overcome the pain. *Weep if you must, rage if you can, but do not let death wound and bind you with its shadows.*

*

Six souls—where are you? Please give us the power to fight. No! In order to rest those souls in peace, I screamed a silent oath to myself. "By the life now gone from those six bodies, we will live, and we swear to continue." With these Sherpas gone, our expedition had now cost eight lives. A strange shadow covered us all. This was a far cry from the joyful ski adventure we had anticipated. There could be no happy ending anymore.

An expedition is a relentless, amoral thing. We witnessed many deaths of people who were not directly involved with our overall purpose, which was to realize an ideal for myself and for the Japanese people.

Many people will probably say we caused the death of those innocent Sherpas. I really don't understand why the Japanese who were at the same spot at the same time were saved. At the exact moment of the tragedy, the ground where Amma and Yassan were standing cracked open. A great block of ice was sucked into the void between them. The rope tieing them together caught underneath the ice, but the great block missed them by less than an inch. They escaped by chopping each other's ropes with picks.

*

Everything surrounding Ohba and Fujise was sucked into the upheaval. The block of ice they were standing on sank, but was not sucked in. They watched the collapse, huddling together. Soga was climbing with one of the best Sherpas. He stopped to rest just before the accident. The Sherpa continued to his death. Dr. Hashimoto had decided to conduct medical experiments with some of the climbers, but his team started a little late, after having to fix some equipment. That delay saved them. I myself had planned to go up there, thinking that I would not be able to see the icefall once I left the train at Shangri-La Glacier, but I didn't get up in time to join the team. I had been writing letters till late the night before.

*

We trembled at the sight of death that the icefall brought. It would be more credible if the attack had been ordered by some commanding officer—if we had some human enemy to hate for his cruelty instead of the expressionless face of nature. Exploration is the same as war—a monstrous game with human lives as chips.

*

To Know Collapse
    Everything can collapse. Houses, bodies, and enemies collapse when their rhythms are deranged.
    When the enemy starts to collapse you must pursue him and not let go. If you fail to take advantage of your enemy's collapse, he may recover and not be so negligent thereafter.
    Watch your enemy's disadvantages accumulate toward collapse, attack unceasingly, and he cannot recover.

MUSASHI "Ring of Fire"

*

Let Us Go Home While We Are Alive

Our team was divided into three groups. One went down to the burial moraine near Lobuje with the bodies of the Sherpas to participate in their funeral. The second continued training and filming at Shangri-La, and the last maintained camp.

While we were training at Shangri-La, the support team at Base Camp found itself in trouble. Don-chan radioed in a desperate voice that he was surrounded by Sherpa women screaming, "Give us back our husbands!" The wives and mothers, the lovers and sisters of the Sherpas who had survived were determined to take their men home by force. "We don't want any money! Just let us go home, while our men are still alive!" The Sherpas looked at the women out of the corners of their eyes without saying a word, and most of them were dragged home. On the way out, some Sherpas told us secretly, "We will escape from them and be back in a week." There were so few who remained that I wondered if we could go on. But if worst came to worst, we would haul the gear by ourselves.

The Sherpa women really believed what the hermit of Khumbila had said, that an evil eastern star dogged this expedition. We could hardly contradict his belief. Although Base Camp was in great trouble, our two weeks of training at Shangri-La was useful. The memory of the tragedy gradually faded away among the Sherpas who remained. I guess that keeping busy and working hard were the best medicine for grief.

We reviewed the videotape recordings of the parachute-opening test, the oxygen system's operations, and the communication system installed in the helmet. The Sherpas were really impressed and said that they had participated in many foreign expeditions, but Japan's was something else. Those two weeks' training were primarily to acclimate the cameramen and the skiers to the altitude. I was able to ski my fill for the first time in a long while. Because of

Blade in the sun. *Photograph copyright © Akira Kotani.*

excitement and overexertion, I returned to Base Camp
completely exhausted.

*

Leaving Base Camp Behind

April 22. In the early morning, Tonko whispered that
somebody with the Japanese Alpine Club had died.
He said that he had heard the news on the transceiver.
No one was supposed to know it, but the information
spread in expanding waves first to the team members and
then to all the Sherpas. I couldn't stand it: Mount Everest
was still asking for victims. We found out that a member of
the Alpine Club of Keio University had died of a heart
attack at 8:45 the previous night at a camp located at
nineteen thousand feet.

Everyone rushed to the doctor's tent for a checkup; nobody had taken personal health seriously up until this point. Yamamoto came back with a long face, saying that he had high blood pressure. I could understand.

There is no other time in life when you lose your confidence and worry as much as when you find out that science has discovered something wrong with your body. There was nothing anybody could do about it in this remote place. Most people have a collection of physical defects which, if ignored, will probably explode some day. Should human beings stay in bed and move around like moles to insure a few extra years of survival? Were we making a mistake risking our precious lives this way? Is it stupid to test the limits of one's power, or is that a road to something sacred? My instinct whispered that once I start, I must keep trying to the last spark of life. I wondered what death was like high on Mount Everest.

*

April 23. At last, we would head for the icefall the next day. I spent all morning straightening out my gear in the tent. In the afternoon I wrote a philosophical article entitled, "At the Starting Point." Then I got a checkup at the medical tent. Blood pressure: 100/130. The left chambers of my heart were a little enlarged, but otherwise I was in perfect shape. I had wanted to write to all those people who had done me favors, including Mr. Akai, but the day had already slipped by. In the evening we tested the telemeter. At bedtime, we attached sensors to my skin to get an electrocardiograph during sleep.

*

April 24. 4:30 A.M. The day had come to negotiate the dreaded icefall. Mr. Zeniya of the filming team and a cameraman were there to film and see us off.

5:30 A.M. Finally, the sun's rise touched the peak of Pumori. It wasn't cold; we didn't even need gloves. I would have preferred the cold, thinking it would be safer without the icefall melting and loosening rocks and blocks of ice.

We had rice mush for breakfast. Mr. Sakai set up the telemeter to check heart-function variations as we climbed from Base Camp at seventeen thousand feet to Camp 1 at nineteen thousand feet. Dr. Nishigori also accompanied us. A very forceful man, he was nicknamed Benkei, a powerful samurai hero in medieval Japan. He commented that he had come not as a doctor but rather as a coolie to carry luggage. He fought with the icefall every day, carrying as much as the Sherpas. Strangely enough, there were a lot of men like him in this team.

*

Strolling Among the Monster's Fangs

We entered the icefall. The tongue of a gigantic demon. The unpredictable ice monster. We began to feel that this was a real expedition. It was absolutely beautiful. We climbed between huge towers and blocks of ice that resembled a broken glass castle. *Is anything else in the world as large as this, so filled with such dangerous fragile beauty?*

I was entranced in this frigid world. No great art work can compare with this huge mass of ice. Its only practical use would be in the highballs of gods and devils.

For people who have an eye and an open heart for beauty, and for those who love mountains, this must be the most wonderful playground in the world. Looking into a crevasse at each step and hearing the occasional musical sound of the groaning glacier, or looking into the dark blue hell at the bottom of the crevasse, tiptoeing over a suspension bridge made of old ropes ready to break, I thought I was in a dangerous paradise.

*

8:00 A.M. On the way to Camp 1, we stopped at a small storage camp. The cameramen Ishiguro and Kanau stayed overnight here last night in order to film our climbing over the icefall. They had their cameras set up in a very dangerous spot. It looked like a battlefield.

Hauling loads. *Photograph copyright © Akira Kotani.*

Crossing a crevasse on the Khumbu Glacier. *Photograph copyright © Kazunari Yasuhisa.*

Fifteen Sherpas in red parkas came down from above the first camp to haul our luggage up. We decided to wait until the team brought Narita's body down. Soon, we could hear the sound of a group of Alpine Club members, including the team captains, coming down with the body. No more, let's not repeat it.

*

After a few silent prayers, we crossed the aluminum bridge, climbed up the ladders, passed through the ice tunnel, and crossed a ragged field of ice blocks—up and up, climbing up. When we looked from the bottom of a wide crevasse, we could see the mountaineers' campsite perched on an imposing wall of ice. After crossing one more crevasse we reached our camp. It was noon.

*

Because I was wearing the sensor and cord of a telemeter on my chest and carried the instrument itself in my backpack, I had to wait for Dr. Nishigori. The medical team was monitoring my pulse by radio. Sakai reported that they could hear me very well at Base Camp over the transceiver. My pulse was 140 maximum, 90 minimum; that was supposed to be pretty good at this height, given that I was carrying thirty-five pounds.

I trained myself, when mountain climbing, not to put too much force into each step. It was better to move like a snail in a place like this and survive than to go too fast and burn out. At this high altitude, where the air was so thin, I seemed to forget things easily—I couldn't keep track of the time. A short break seemed to stretch into a lazy hour unnoticed. Of course, it could be due to the beautiful scenery and the surroundings. I was never bored looking at them.

My Shinto ancestors saw each mountain as a god. They were not pagans; they knew that the mountains were just as much deified by the presence of humans as the other way around. But the high clarity of mountain peaks, with their sweeping vistas of forests, rice fields, and villages, all living and growing and seeding and dying, put my ancestors in touch with the essential unity of life, and for that gift of vision they worshiped the mountains.

*

Love at First Sight

April 25. In the Western Cwm. Camp 1. Weather clear. First night at nineteen thousand feet. It was a little hard to breathe last night. I ate two big bowls of food for dinner. I wondered if that was too much. But I got hungry in the middle of the night. The next morning, to get myself used to the altitude, I decided to take a walk up to Camp 2, the Advance Base Camp at twenty thousand feet.

*

Kanau, the cameraman, was waiting for me with a smile. We explored the area for nearly an hour, and finally came to the golden—no, the platinum—road, with the summit of Everest on the left, Lhotse straight ahead, and Nuptse on the right. Mesmerized, I climbed up the big snow field, my gaze transfixed by the power and beauty of the view. I could see my ski route gleaming. That wall of ice leading up to Everest looked like a frozen, silver waterfall pouring beside the Western Cwm.

*

The course looks much better than I had ever imagined or heard. "I think it will be a wonderful downhill," I reassured myself. From the previous year, I remembered it as a very broad and open slope. I had trembled a little when I decided to ski that line, as if I had just challenged God to a duel. But now it seemed a little smaller, a little more feasible. I was worried that there would be a band of rocks across the narrow middle section, but it was fully covered with snow there.

My heart felt lighter. With all the crevasses at my feet I could not walk looking up all the time and, so, tore my eyes away. In all the world I don't think I could find another path as wonderful as this. The land was pure white on the surface, and blue and black inside the crevasses. The clouds were tinged with a dozen colors, gently surrounding and setting off the mountain. Compared to last year—maybe because it was now pre-monsoon season—the mountain looked a little thinner—pale and dry, with a cold, cruel beauty.

*

Our Advance Camp was pitched at twenty thousand feet, at the western edge of Mount Everest, near a blue-striped icefall. Kanau and I called out as loud as we could, but there was no one there. It was just like a ghost town. Probably, everybody was hauling equipment up to Camp 3. It was very hot inside the tent—we took off all our clothes, but we were still hot. It was like a sauna. We switched on our radio and contacted Amma at Base Camp. "All clear," we said to each other.

*

The General Knows His Troops
    Using the wisdom of strategy, treat the enemy as you would your own troops. Move him at will, let him know you are in command, not he.

MUSASHI "Ring of Fire"

*

"Half Strike"

April 26. Clear in the morning, cloudy in the afternoon. This was supposed to be the typical weather pattern of the pre-monsoon season. Wraithy mists billowed continuously from the bottom of the southern icefall every afternoon. I climbed halfway up to the Advance Base Camp with Kanau and some other cameramen and skied on a slope in the middle of a rocky ridge on Nuptse.

We quickly realized why the Sherpas called this spot dangerous. When we mentioned yesterday that it was a great spot for skiing, we couldn't understand why the Sherpas whispered among themselves and shook their heads, but now we found out—it was raining rocks. It might be the greatest spot in the world for ski movies and photographs, but we didn't want to become the victims of whizzing, eighty-mile-an-hour rock cannonades. We skied through the area fast, feeling as if we were under enemy fire.

On our return to Camp 1, we were too lazy to take off our skis, so we just decided to slide, clinging to the rope across the aluminum bridge and sliding down the vertical wall. The Sherpas couldn't believe their eyes.

*

We decided to attack the South Col on April 29. The final act would occur any day between May 5 and May 7, probably the sixth.

We speeded up the pace of gear hauling, but the Sherpas grew weary from the hard work every day. The altitude made everything increasingly difficult. The luggage for the next day was particularly heavy. It was too much. The Sherpas in our party were loyal and friendly, but the Sherpas in Camp 1, especially those with stubby legs, complained that with heavy packs they could not step over the crevasses.

Some of the team members tried to convince the Sherpas to work harder instead. I listened from the tent next door, and it was really funny: "You people may be short and small, but you eat five and six bowls of food at a time, and you can't even manage this puny seventy pounds of luggage." The Sherpas were silent. That evening, thirteen Sherpas said they would not eat. They said the captain had hurt their feelings. "The captain said we eat five or six bowls of rice, but it is only about three, even when we eat a lot," they grumbled. "If that's what you think, we're not going to eat any food at all. We'll work, but only half as hard, and we're going to tell Don-chan when we reach the Advance Base Camp tomorrow that we have gone on half strike." The nightly mumble of Sherpa prayers was absent that evening. Perhaps they had lost their voices from hunger.

*

Soba Noodles at 19,500 Feet

April 27. Cameraman Yano, who was sleeping in the tent next to the Sherpas, said that he had found it very noisy last night. It sounded as if all the Sherpas were chewing on pilot biscuits. The Sherpas took their packs and started the climb without saying a word this morning.

*

I woke from a relaxed sleep and got up at 6:00 A.M. The sky had looked ominous last night, and this morning it was unusually cloudy. The sun was barely visible. Later in the morning the clouds disappeared. As the sun rose higher, the tent turned into an oven. Though the wind was cool outside, direct sunlight could broil your skin. I put some wax on my leather ski boots; it melted instantly, just like butter. No wonder my face got so red. When I took off my clothes, I got burned on the sunny side, while frostbite hit the shady side.

*

Otaki prepared some delicious Japanese *soba* noodles—a kind of brown spaghetti. We sat on a cardboard box outside the tent and ate very noisily.

Afterwards, we found a nice jump platform near a crevasse. One morning, after I woke from a nap, I found Tadano jumping, while Kanau and Otaki snapped photographs with great excitement. I joined them. My timing was so good I could float in the air with only about half of Tadano's approach. Once I launched so perfectly that I flew too far and fell spread-eagled onto the ice.

It became too cloudy for either photographing or filming, but still we exercised and jumped. Come to think of it, I don't think I ever tried as hard on the ski slopes in the world down below. I didn't feel tired. When I was out of breath, I recovered quickly. "All I have to do is to make sure I don't overdo it. If I'm careful, I can easily climb up to twenty-six thousand feet, or maybe even to the top!" I told myself.

Flying high in the Himalayas. *Phogograph copyright © Akira Kotani.*

*

To Injure the Corners
   It is difficult to move heavy objects all at once. In war it is wise to
strike first at the corners of an equal or superior enemy force. Once the
corners are destroyed, the spirit of the main body will more easily
crumble. You must press home your advantage once the corners have
collapsed, or the centers will reconsolidate.

MUSASHI "Ring of Fire"

*

Those Who Sleep Better Live Better

April 28. The weather was clear at Camp 1, but it turned
cloudy by nine o'clock. I slept well, but still had to get up
to go to the "bathroom" twice around midnight. The doctor
kept telling me to drink water. He said at high altitudes one
quickly becomes dehydrated. I felt like a giant frog drinking
entire lakes of liquid.

*

When the Sherpas rose at six o'clock, I left the tent for a stroll. Though the weather was clear, somehow the day felt threatening. There was the usual cloud stampede around the top of Mount Everest, but this morning across the crowns of all the mountains, Pumori, Lhotse, and Nuptse, you could see the long trailing plumes of snow which indicate high winds.

*

Exercise is best before breakfast, especially if all you have to eat are instant noodles. Most of the team members who ate first and immediately went climbing with heavy packs usually ended up vomiting along the way. Instead, I drank black tea with garlic, honey with royal jelly, and extract of Ginseng root for breakfast. I don't normally take vitamin pills, but because I had heard that vitamin E was helpful at high altitudes, I took about twenty a day. It was an odd diet, but at least it was better than "minute" rice and instant noodles. I also ate what the Sherpas eat—potatoes and *tsamba*. Careful to avoid a lack of vitamin C, I made tea in the cup by throwing a handful of leaves directly into boiling water. I drank the tea and also ate the tea leaves that were soft and tender. I ate lots of seaweed and dried fish; no iodine deficiency for me!

*

I skied without breakfast and thoroughly enjoyed it, even though the snow was hard and a monstrous crevasse lay a little too close. It was scary, skiing below a great wall of Himalayan wrinkles, with wavy snow, jagged ice, and dark blue crevasses underfoot, but the cameramen were excited, my body felt light, and I had no trouble breathing. Skiing today felt even better than it had a few days before in Shangri-La. My muscle tone was the best of my life. I felt as enthused as at the beginning of ski season, when new snow robes my ancestral mountains at Tateyama and Hakoda in Japan.

Still, I couldn't ski for very long, or rather I should say

Playing on the deadly edge. *Photograph copyright © Akira Kotani.*

that it did not feel good for my body. Two hours was my limit after that.

At high altitudes there is a sudden turning point, like a switch which has been flicked off suddenly. You can feel the energy draining from your body. This signifies not only exhaustion of the muscles, but of the brain as well. When the muscles grow weak, the mind gets sloppy.

*

After a short nap I decided to continue the jumping I had started the day before. I was even able to try an "air snake," a difficult jump, the trick of which is to keep your balance while you move the ends of your skis in the air like a snake. Even at lower altitudes it's hard, but I jumped about sixteen feet and easily maneuvered the skis in the air. I kept doing it from three o'clock to five o'clock without stopping, until I finally lost consciousness in mid-air. I just fell asleep during a jump and crash landed. I decided to stop.

*

The weather started to clear and the clouds grew gentle and thin, as if to take the veils off the mountains. I guess the low atmospheric pressure was gone. Don-chan and Yassan were already up at Camp 4. At last, tomorrow we'll be heading for the South Col. *Let's put up a good fight.* At night in the tent I watched my jumping on the videotape recorder.

*

Tired Brain

April 29. There was a great wind last night. The skis which I had leaned against the tent had blown down, and I went outside to secure them. It worried me—this strange weather with lots of clouds. I wondered if it was because of the wind or because of the quantities of tea I had drunk since early afternoon that I could not fall asleep. Nine, ten, eleven o'clock. Dozing off here and there. Eleven-thirty. I could not keep track of the time, but finally morning came.

The lack of sleep had exhausted my brain. And today, Oh yes! Today I was supposed to go to the Advance Base Camp to straighten out the equipment.

*

The wind was too strong. There would be hard work for Don-chan and his party at the South Col. Left by myself, with no rope or Sherpas to accompany me, I took a shortcut by climbing all the way down to the bottom of a crevasse and climbing back up an icy face. My head was numb and rubbery, and I found it hard to breathe. In about fifteen minutes I caught up with Ishiguro and Kanau, passed them, and kept going by myself. I could really feel the effects of the altitude. Even the backpack, which weighed only twenty-two pounds, felt very heavy.

*

Still, this was easy compared to last year—that was really something. Last year, the day after I arrived at Camp 1, I put poorly fitting sealskins on my skis. They slipped off every time I pushed too hard or took a diagonal traverse. I had to stop and put them back on every five minutes. At that time, I was packing forty-four pounds on my back, a load even Sherpas didn't want to carry.

Trying to climb up the Western Cwm on skis, I thought I would die from exhaustion. I finally had dropped all my luggage and staggered up to the Advance Base Camp. I slept like a slug after I crawled into the tent. Anyway, I had put up a fight.

Later I found out that at such a high altitude 1 pound on your feet is equivalent to 7 pounds carried on your back. That means that skis at 11 pounds and boots at 5 pounds would be equivalent to 105 pounds. When you add what was on my back—44 pounds—it amounted to my carrying about 150 pounds, without knowing it, and at an altitude of nineteen thousand feet.

*

"Considering what I've gone through, I ought to be able to climb to the top of Everest without oxygen," I mumbled to myself last year. This year I said, "This is the best walking road I could ever find in the world," as I strode up the wide, white desert amid little cracks threatening to open into chasms and occasional stones whizzing and whistling down the icy slopes.

*

Pushing Higher Altitudes

My spirits rose. I came to a plateau where I could see the Advance Base Camp village high above me. Thinking that it wouldn't even take me an hour and a half with this little backpack, I tried to make a race of it. Normally, it would take about three to four hours, because I'd rest along the way. The Sherpas who left with me had long since disappeared behind.

I have a very strange habit of trying to win bets with myself, whether it's a new personal record or not. Usually it's just a bet in my heart, so it does not bother anybody else. But it bothers me if I lose.

That day, knowing my physical condition wasn't the best, I shouldn't have tried it, but I decided to try to increase my speed anyway. I felt like an old car with a steaming radiator. Suddenly, I grew very weak. I supposed this was the evil influence of high altitude in the Himalayas. It was not dangerous now, to collapse in good weather with companions ahead and behind, but suppose this had happened in a snowstorm or a difficult section of the route? I learned something. I learned for myself the reason for tragedies in the Himalayas.

Still, I kept pushing myself. *It is not a good thing to give up something in the middle.*

*

I was mad at the tents for not coming closer. With oxygen in short supply, I decided to set my pace based upon the work of the busiest organ of my body, the lungs. I said, "Okay, body, a hundred more breaths, and you get to rest."

When you are tired, you start to breathe faster, which

enables you to inhale more air, and this keeps the muscles fueled with oxygen. I found that when your rhythm of breathing matches your pace, you don't tire as fast and recover more quickly.

I practiced breathing loudly in the caravan to try to synchronize the two rhythms. I begin to breathe that way naturally when engaged in hard training, so when I go to the mountains or exercise with people who do not really know me, they always think that I am already exhausted from the start and look at me with surprise. Of course there are times when I really am tired from the beginning, but then nobody can tell the difference. I don't practice exaggerated breathing when I ski because it upsets the delicate balance.

However, today, I just made a lot of noise; there was no power or energy in my breathing. I failed to reach my destination within an hour and a half and reprimanded myself.

*

When I arrived at the camp of the Japanese Alpine Club, about a hundred yards below our Advance Base Camp, I accepted their insistent invitations and sat down on their only aluminum chair and had some tea. I talked idly with them, and, since it was already noon, accepted their offer of lunch. I was getting so comfortable, I was afraid I'd be eating dinner there too, so I decided to leave. I thanked them and left for our Advance Base Camp. It was only a little hill with a very gentle grade, but I ended up panting.

*

Transfer
    Many feelings are transferred unconsciously, like sleepiness and yawning. Timing, too, is transferred this way.
    When the enemy is excited and ready to spring, do not mind in the least. Infect him with a show of serenity. The feeling will transfer, and the enemy will relax. At that moment, attack from the Void, give him no chance to re-prepare.

MUSASHI "Ring of Fire"

*

I hauled my skis toward camp. *Photograph copyright © Akira Kotani.*

Bright News

The tent village of our Advance Base Camp reminded me of a Spanish patio surrounded by blocks of ice and snow. Japanese and Nepalese flags slapped in the wind, and a small arch of little flags made a welcoming gate. In the center of camp was a little altar of snow blocks, and the tents were pitched comfortably around it like prostrate monks in a reverie. The camp was complete with a small bathroom of ice blocks outside the circle, and another one inside the area for lighter business.

*

One by one, the team members came in. I heard that our South Col team had finally reached its goal. Too bad I can't say that they were the first Japanese; a day earlier two men from the Japanese Alpine Club had already reached there. I understand our men had already set up a tent at the South Col and transported all our luggage up there. Five Sherpas without oxygen hauled thirty-two pounds each. Don-chan and Yassan used oxygen for safety, but only half the time.

This was happy news. Everybody bubbled with excitement. Looking through the telescope, we could already see our team traversing down the ice face of Lhotse and passing the Yellow Band. They looked smaller than flecks of dust against the great slope. In the evening, a cumulus cloud hovered above the peak of Pumori on the far side of the valley. Sometimes it looked like a noble human face, while at others, a grinning monster.

*

April 30: At the Advance Base Camp, 21,125 feet above sea level, I woke in the middle of the night feeling hungry. I guess three bowls of Japanese noodles were not quite enough.

This day was supposed to be for rest and preparation, so I crawled back into my sleeping bag after breakfast, but I quickly became bored. "Should I move around or stay in bed? Which will help blood circulation and body conditioning best? Will I get altitude sickness if I ski in this condition, or should I start getting used to quick action at this elevation?" I thought about it for a while and decided to move around. If that didn't work, I could always go back to sleep.

*

I started climbing with my skis on my shoulder. I could feel the blood moving like cold molasses. Though it was painful, I drove myself and continued to climb, working on the rhythm of my breathing. "Don't give up immediately. Walk for at least thirty minutes," I told myself.

As my blood began to thin, I was able to climb comfortably. My breathing came alive. I skied the whole morning, jumping and turning, to the cameramen's delight.

*

Don-chan came back from South Col with a great smile. I decided to wait till tonight to hear his story. Anticipating good news is often as good as the news itself, and it usually lasts a lot longer. Hungry after skiing, I ate two great bowlfuls of food for lunch and then took a nap as planned, but the heat in the tent was unbearable. I stuck my neck and the upper part of my body into the shade outside the tent, leaving my naked legs sealed up inside. I slept very well. After I woke up, I skied some more to get used to the altitude.

*

Yesterday, three Sherpas, Tadano, and I put a lot of effort into building a jump platform. Seen from the side, it looked as if I would have to jump about sixty feet, sailing all the way over the tent. With the great downhill still to come, I cautioned myself not to do anything silly and get hurt. I hesitated, but since I felt so good, I decided to jump anyway. It was a great jump, and the platform was excellent. At the cameramen's request, I repeated it about twenty times. Some thirty Sherpas, including Girmi Dorje and Ang Pema, who had just come back completely exhausted from the South Col, gawked in amazement. All the men from the Alpine Club watched, too. Tadano and I took turns jumping.

We especially enjoyed flying over the tent and watching the Sherpas stare open-mouthed like hungry fish. We didn't stop until we began to get numb. The sun had already started to set behind the shadow of Cho Oyu. I was amazed that I could do such things at twenty-one thousand feet.

*

In the evening in our tent, gathered around captains Don-chan and Yassan, were Amma, Hashimoto, Kotani, Kanau, Otaki, Ishiguro, Tadano, Ajisaka, and myself. I wonder how we were able to fit so many people in that little tent. We listened and talked about our plans and experiences so far. We laughed so hard our stomachs began to ache. The overall condition of our team was excellent. According to Don-chan, the members of our team were just like "employees of a company on its way up!" *It's high tide—let's sail with the energy!*

*

May 1: Strong winds, but clear. My head aches from laughter and lack of sleep. With so many people in one tent, we had burned about ten candles all at once. Cameraman Kotani, who was sleeping next to me, was moaning from a headache. I got up, but my body felt as if it were made of clay. I was supposed to test my parachute today, but just going to the bathroom was an effort. The doctor said it was from overexertion the day before.

*

In the afternoon, we all watched the videotape cassettes of our families back in Tokyo. The most popular face was the wife of cameraman Kotani. The Sherpas said, "Kotani *sabu* face no good, wife good!" Kotani, whose face was a pair of glasses floating in the middle of a great field of beard, smiled.

Dr. Yoda's beautiful sister was another hit. Thinking that Nepal, being west of Japan, must be full of Westerners, she said, "I hope you will come back with a blue-eyed

Peaceful candlelight and camaraderie. *Photograph copyright © Akira Kotani.*

wife." Some team members debated whether or not there were any blue-eyed girls who would be a match for the doctor. Dr. Yoda was only five foot two.

*

The Great Crevasse in the Downhill Course

May 2. We left camp to scout around the area of the Bergschrund, the great crevasse below the gleaming ice wall of the South Col. We heard that the Bergschrund was very bare this year, but never thought it could be as bad as this. It was an evil, gaping mouth that cut across the base of the icefalls from Everest, Lhotse and Nuptse. At 22,425 feet, the crevassed Bergschrund was fearsomely wide. It looked like a ravenous snake, waiting to swallow anything that fell from the sky or snow above. I would be coming down that way in a very few days.

*

The tumbled mass of debris inside the crevasse looked like a big city after an earthquake. The bottom of the crevasse was dark and sunken, as if it led to the bottom of hell itself. "Where can I get through it? It will be impossible to come to a stop above the crevasse, even if the parachute opens." The angle of the slope got steeper and steeper as it approached the Bergschrund. Except for one narrow strip of snow, the whole area was one big shiny ice chute, like polished steel. Even an ice pick would be useless. If I wanted to make a painting of despair, this would be it. "At least find an escape route," I implored myself.

*

There appeared to be a way through. I could see a small white spot below the Geneva Spur, which jutted out like the beak of a bird. White could mean snow. If I could maneuver into that area and manage to brake in that white spot with both the parachute and my ski edges, then I could turn toward the snow slope pitched at thirty degrees which skirted the narrow left side of the crevasse. Once there, I might be able to get out with a rope. There was no other choice. I also thought about going toward Lhotse, but considering the wind and the ugly, icy conditions, that seemed even worse.

How would I ever be able to find that tiny white spot—perhaps five yards wide—from thousands of feet above it? Against the gleaming white glacial background, it would be like looking for a needle dropped in the desert. Not much of a chance, but still, it was much better than no chance at all. Anyway, what a wonderful icefall!

*

To Penetrate the Depths
    It is not enough to defeat an enemy if his spirit remains defiant. You must penetrate the depths of your enemy's spirit and utterly destroy him. Crush him completely or he will return to harass you.
                                        MUSASHI "Ring of Fire"

*

Miura, Kanau and Don-chan study the ski course. *Photograph copyright © Akira Kotani.*

Camp at the Evil Altitude

May 3. I woke up in the middle of the night. Eleven o'clock, one o'clock, two o'clock—I couldn't sleep—not from fear of the slope, but from a kind of nervous excitement. Maybe it was the noisy winds outside, or maybe it was the gathering storm of destiny, howling in the predawn light of days soon to come.

I read that Lindbergh was unable to sleep the night before he flew to Paris, but I couldn't sleep even four days before my feat.

In the morning I ate three big bowls of rice mush. I was half asleep from eating too much. This was a day for climbing, but I felt too heavy to move. However, when everyone started to leave, I was ready in a flash and left with an ice ax in my hand and crampons on my boots.

Today we moved up from Advance Base Camp to

Camp 3, located at 22,587 feet. I've heard that even Sherpas, if they've never been this high before, get mountain sickness. This is supposed to be the hardest altitude to handle.

Below this point it was not too bad, but twenty-two thousand feet was said to be the dividing line. For some, the pain could be the torment of hell. Even with a mild case of altitude sickness, you get a headache that feels like a metal ring tightening around your skull.

"It's not all that bad," said Don-chan, the superman. Even in my bad condition, if I walked steadily, I would get to Camp 3 sometime.

I managed to pass everybody else and arrived within an hour and forty minutes, right behind Don-chan. I didn't even feel any nausea.

The campsite stood at the base of an ice precipice, below the slope of Lhotse, which looked so fragile that it might start crumbling anytime. A rope dangled down the precipice. Just the thought of climbing on it tomorrow made me feel tired.

*

As I lay napping in the tent, I was brought some oxygen equipment. I examined the vinyl and polyethylene oxygen mask, which was like those used on commercial passenger planes, and found it very light. I didn't really need it, but my curiosity was aroused. I regulated the flow to one quart per minute, since I had been told that between a half and one quart per minute would be perfect for sleeping. Upon counting my pulse, I found that within two or three minutes it had gone down from ninety to seventy. I felt rather silly using oxygen alone, but told myself this also was a part of my duty to insure a successful expedition.

I was sleeping before I knew it, floating in dreamless peace, when suddenly I felt as if my face were being forced underwater. I choked violently. The mask was dripping wet, moisture poured into my nostrils and mouth. The water came from the accumulated vapor of my breathing. Great system—perfect, for keeping you awake. Furious, I ripped off the mask and turned off the tank.

*

Amateur Rock Climber Goes to Work

May 4. Clear. Heading for Camp 4, set at an altitude of 24,115 feet. After the snowfall last night, the Sherpas were having a hard time. There was only about two inches of powder, but the hard-cut ice steps were covered with snow. The Sherpas had to brush the powder off each step as they climbed. Furthermore, the snow stuck to their boots and crampons, making it very easy to slip. From here on up, the only team members were Don-chan, Yassan, Otaki, Ishiguro and myself, plus the South Col Sherpa Girmi Dorje, and Ang Pema, the strongest of all the Sherpas. Eight other high porters would carry the necessary baggage and equipment up to the South Col.

*

The icewall demanded total concentration. From here on, there was no room for mistakes. Each step, from handling the ropes and the ice ax, to adhering to all the techniques and following the rules of basic mountain safety, demanded precise execution. At the very moment that I was thinking this, the point of my ice ax popped out of the ice, and I nearly fell off the face.

I began to get used to the perpendicular wall and continued to climb for about an hour. To my surprise, the two cameramen, Otaki and Ishiguro, carrying those boulder-sized 35-mm Cinema-Scope cameras, were climbing above me while I clung to the ropes. They kept saying, "Hold on a minute, Mr. Miura, we would like to shoot from above. Smile." Luckily my climbing partner was Genius Yassan, one of the finest rock climbers of Japan, but he too had turned into a mountain cameraman, standing at the head of the rope,

Hauling equipment. *Photograph copyright © Kazunari Yasuhisa.*

taking photographs and requesting different poses: "Mr. Miura, stop for minute. Look up here. Look courageous."

*

I wonder what they were in their previous lives? Don-chan, for instance; he strolled up the face without a rope and had already disappeared into the distance. On this great icewall at twenty-two thousand feet, had they come to destroy the myth of Mount Everest? They didn't even use oxygen. Weren't they panting and feeling the pain? To be honest, I had never learned hard rock or ice climbing. I had been to many mountains, but most of them were for skiing. This was my first experience with fixed ropes. I didn't want to start asking questions now, because nobody would want to team up with me, fearing I might pull them off in a panic.

*

Monkey see, monkey do. I became an instant climber. All right, tie a rope this way—put a carabiner on—oops, I

Sherpa on the Western Cwm. *Photograph copyright © Kazunari Yasuhisa.*

have forgotten the carabiner. "Ishiguro, could I borrow one
of your spares?" Then clip it on the rope. How do I open it?
Let's mark it with colored tape for easy identification. I don't
think anybody in history was a slower rock climber than I.
At this rate, I don't think any sane person would want to
rope up with me, even on a staircase.

*

I wonder what I was in my last life? Sherpas keep
saying behind my back that I was a *yeti* or a *choti* in a
previous incarnation. After a while, climbing this vertical
wall began to feel rather comfortable. At first I was very
nervous, crawling around tensely, clinging to the rope, but
gradually I found myself trying to pose, as if I were a first-
class mountain climber.

Genius, true to his reputation, was a fine mountain
climber. Even climbing with his camera, he did everything
with swift certainty.

I began to understand the difference between danger and difficulty. Danger can't be helped by technique or effort, only handled when it arises. But difficulties can be overcome with discipline, by scoffing at the laziness of heart which tries to escape the sweat and suffering that develop ability.

*

The earth spread open before us. I could see the icy peaks, which we had thought so high, begin to appear one by one at our feet. I could see the wall of ice as I climbed, that wall of ice I was supposed to ski down in two days. What kind of man would ski in such a place? Is he a god? A madman? I am awed and terrified by myself. Is it true that I'm going there? What will it feel like when I pass that point? How can I get around that rock? What can I do to avoid falling into that crevasse? No matter how I look at it, it doesn't seem real. It is like some fantasy from another world, far, far away. I continued to climb.

*

At the fourth camp were three little pin points that dotted two wrinkles inside the fourth finger of Lhotse's icewall. The icy wall stood like a hand held vertically, as if to say, "You cannot pass!" Our three tents were little birds' nests on the icy cliffs. They were only a few inches from the edge, barely clinging to the precipice.

One wrong step, and you would fall like a stone thousands of feet into Camp 3 or into the Bergschrund, which looked like a devil yawning in foul temper. This was not a world for human beings.

*

Steps to Glory

May 5: Clear. Strong wind. In order not to disturb Camp 4's precarious perch, we were very careful starting out for the South Col. The steep slope was difficult and dangerous. An awful wind blew flurries of snow down from

Our three tents were little birds' nests on the icy cliffs.
Photograph copyright © Akira Kotani.

above, stinging our faces with cold, hard crystals. Upon
reaching the Yellow Band, we found Otaki and Ishiguro,
again dragging their cameras, shooting from above and
below—"Please, Mr. Miura, could you hang from that
rope?" They were as casual as they might be in a Hollywood
studio.

*

Beginning today, all of us were using oxygen masks and
carrying tanks, as planned. We were just like children
waiting for cookies. I don't think it made a critical
difference, but it did make the climbing easier. Two liters
per minute—this was twice what we used when sleeping,
but still only half the amount of oxygen we breathe in the
world below. I felt very comfortable, even more comfortable
than climbing at twelve thousand feet on Mount Fuji.

My relaxed attitude came from concentrating on my

ultimate goal. I am not pretending—this is the pride of a knight challenging something huge—the samurai spirit.

*

All the first-class men of the world have climbed here—Hillary, Lambert, Tensing. These are the steps of glory on Mount Everest. Footsteps on the Geneva Spur have marked a quarter century of climbing. Only a few men have traveled this route headed for the South Col. They have left footsteps of glory and retreat. As for me, I will not walk this path again. I will be taking a different road tomorrow.

*

To Crush
  If the enemy is weak, if his rhythm is poor, if he has fallen into evasive tactics, knock his hat over his eyes and crush him all at once. Give his future no concern. Allow him no space for breath.

MUSASHI "Ring of Fire"

*

The World's Highest Dump

This is a very high place, the highest campground in the world: Mount Everest, the South Col, twenty-six thousand feet above sea level. The South Col is depressingly bleak. In the fall of 1952, the Swiss expedition turned back at this point, saying they could smell death. It's been called the most desolate spot on earth. The U.S. expedition called it the highest garbage dump in the world. Be that as it may, I was glad enough when I finally got there.

Though I had never been on the South Col before, I felt the kind of nostalgia that pilgrims enjoy when they finally reach the promised land. I wandered around in the screaming wind.

*

Indeed, it was the world's highest garbage dump. It was full of trash left by explorers of the past: oxygen tanks with needles pointed to zero among the rocks, pieces of string and cloth, the shredded remains of tents, still flapping in the wind. Kerosene stoves, old transmitters, candles, parkas,

Survival at high elevations is not easy. *Photograph copyright © Akira Kotani.*

masks—I don't know how these things stayed put with the constant wind, but here they were, clinging to the rocks. Soon ours would join them.

*

Our tent, set up only a week ago, was only a step away from collapsing. It flapped like a runaway kite, abused by the brutal wind. I took off the oxygen mask I had worn since Camp 4. Because I could concentrate only on withstanding the gale-force winds, I couldn't tell if I were suffering from lack of oxygen or not. It did not even occur to me that the amount of oxygen here was only one-third of that in the world below. I was breathing the thin air without the mask, but I couldn't tell the difference.

When I left Base Camp, I had jokingly boasted of standing on my head when I reached the South Col. It was possible, of course, but the wind would have blown me right into the rocks—and over the side.

I rummaged around the outside of the tent, thinking there might still be something useful among the debris. It was nothing to be proud of, but I must have been the world's highest garbage collector. Of course, all the worthwhile objects had already been taken by our senior garbage collectors, the Sherpas. They had gone through the garbage five years ago when they were here with the American explorers.

*

Garbage in the Sunset

I am a little embarrassed to say that I was busier going through the garbage on the ground than being impressed by the grand scenery. Except for Everest, the mountains which usually gave us stiff necks from looking up were now below us. We could almost touch their tops, but many of them had already hidden their heads behind the clouds.

*

Sunset was late in coming. Because we were so high—close to the top of the earth—we could see nearly a full circle before the sun disappeared beneath the horizon. Twilight kept spreading over the sea of clouds until almost eight o'clock, when it finally grew dark. I wandered around till then. The mountain cameramen—Genius Yassan, Otaki, and Ishiguro—had been there too, shooting the sunset from the world's highest "scenic turnout."

*

The wind bellowed and beat on the tent. Sherpa Ang Pema was melting ice for supper. Don-chan, Kato, and Sherpa Girmi Dorje had not returned from their trip preparing the starting point for the downhill event. Having nothing to do gave me more time to pick through the rubbish. I ended up turning over all the rocks, collecting pitons, until I was convinced I hadn't missed any. I was very successful. I gave them away later as mementos to my colleagues and friends. I thought about taking the empty oxygen tanks too, but at fifteen pounds each, they were too bulky and heavy.

I am probably the most happy-go-lucky fellow who ever made it up to the South Col. Who knows, I might even be applauded by the Himalayan Environmental Sanitation Department for cleaning up the area.

I am not trying to brag, but I didn't use my oxygen tank at all during this activity. I wasn't the only one: Don-chan ran out of oxygen on his way back from setting up two-hundred-foot lengths of thick rope at tomorrow's starting point. He came back from rock climbing at twenty-six thousand feet with no trouble and was amazed at himself.

*

Blown into Tibet

Tibetans say the air is evil up here. Fortunately, it did not seem to hurt us, the five team members who were spending our first night here. Oxygen helped, but I imagine we could have survived without it.

The Sherpas were incredibly strong. They may have complained afterward, but they came all the way up here without the help of oxygen, carrying thirty- to forty-five-pound loads. Thinking of my own experience, I don't know how they managed; they performed their tasks under enormous stress.

*

We tried to communicate by transceiver with other camps, but the wind was so noisy we couldn't hear. Besides, it would have been too much trouble to deliver anything we might have forgotten. We had to remove our oxygen masks when speaking into the microphone, and we lost our breath just trying to shout. Even talking to somebody right next to you was too much of a struggle. I turned off the switch on the transceiver.

We didn't communicate till eight o'clock the following morning because of the shrieking wind; also, everybody slept late the next morning. Nobody even got out of bed until six-thirty.

We heard later that the people at Base Camp were seriously concerned, saying that the South Col team might have been blown off into Tibet—tents, packs and everything. Not knowing about all these worries, we five Japanese and two Sherpas were quite contented, drinking Ovaltine probably left over from the last Indian expedition. It was at least five years old, and if it came from the Swiss team, it was almost twenty years old.

*

Don-chan looked for a deck of cards. He even went to the next tent, calling out, "Where are the cards?" But he couldn't find any. He was really disappointed; he wanted to set a record for the highest gambling game in the world. Those people—they would probably play cards on the moon.

*

We had mush for supper; I ate two big bowls of it, with some kelp and pickled fish. Then I ate another serving, just so I wouldn't have to wake up in the middle of the night feeling hungry. I asked if there wasn't anything better, but really, if the food were too good up here, we would probably lose interest in getting back to the world below. The worse the food tastes and the more suffering we go through, the happier we will be to get back home. Since we couldn't change the menu, I simply changed my outlook and stopped complaining about the food. *Take what you get; there is nothing else.*

Some schools of fighting hold that you should fix your eyes on the enemy's sword. Some say fix your eyes on the hands. Some say the face, some say the feet, and so on. If you fix your eyes on any place, your spirit can become confused and your strategy destroyed.

In combat you must not fix your eyes on details. The gaze should be broad, viewing distant events as if they were close and nearby events as if they were distant. *Perception* and *sight* are the two techniques for seeing. Perception is strong; it can comprehend the enemy's spirit and the flow and timing of events. Sight is weak; it merely reports changes in appearance.

In mastering the Way of strategy, once you learn to see the weight of your enemy's spirit, you will easily appraise the speed and position of his sword. In strategy, seeing means perceiving the heart of the enemy.

A spirit of controlled command will keep your timing perfect.

MUSASHI "Ring of Wind"

5

The Day
Has Come

MAY 6. South Col. I was determined to be well rested for
the great descent tomorrow. There was a strong, noisy wind
again tonight, so I took some sleeping pills. It was only half
the usual dosage, but because I had never taken them
before, I slept like a pig. The Sherpas complained that they
had headaches last night. Because I couldn't find any
aspirin, I gave them the same pills, saying it was good
medicine. They almost passed out on the spot.

I never saw a stronger wind than this. Even when it
calmed, it still blew the tent wall into my face. Occasionally,
the wind let up a little—perhaps it, too, gets tired.

*

My oxygen equipment worked well. It only fouled once
that night. Genius mumbled, "If it leaks, all you do is hit it
a couple of times." Then he whacked the connection
between the regulator and the tank with a big wrench. No
more problems.

*

The wind was still not calm enough for us to work
outside. Inside the tent, I checked out my parachute, oxygen

tank, helmet transceiver, ski boots, poles, and skis, and sharpened my ski edges, just in case. I had already done the whole job once at Advance Base Camp, but I wanted to make doubly sure. I managed to finish all this without jamming the ski poles into the tent wall. Genius sat photographing me, a wry smile on his muscled face.

*

I drank some more Ovaltine. At twenty-six thousand feet, it was delicious. When I asked where I could get more, somebody said, "Probably in India." It seemed like too much trouble to go over there just to buy some for tomorrow.

I took out some thin Japanese towels which I had put in my luggage before leaving Japan and said, "This is from the mountain gods of Japan." Then I wrote in English and in Japanese, "Japan Mount Everest Ski Expedition Team," and included all the names of the Sherpas and team members. I took out a mirror measuring about six-by-eight inches— a little large to carry to the mountains, but a very good one. "Chomolungma, goddess mother of the world, has not had any mirrors before. I think she, as a female, needs a mirror. I hope she'll be happy to have this one."

I marched into the strong wind outside. There was a great boulder in front of the tent, so I gathered some rocks and built a cairn. I placed the mirror between the rocks in such a way that I could see the top of the mountain in its reflection, and laid the towel alongside. I figured that I wouldn't need my ice ax anymore because I'd be skiing down, so I stood the ax among the rocks, and tied on the flags of Japan, Nepal, and our ski expedition team. I didn't know whether they would last for more than half a day in this wind. When the flags were flapping, looking very gay, I felt as if I had accomplished some delicate ceremony. I should have brought something that belonged to those dead Sherpas. *If I die, this is my tomb.*

I realized I was doing all this without oxygen. Strangely, it was not strenuous at all. For safety's sake, I went back to the tent to inhale some.

I asked Sherpa Ang Pema to carry my equipment for the final act. Don-chan and Girmi Dorje had already headed off to the starting point for the downhill.

*

My ancestors saw life as a river with no beginning and no end. Every entity—every person, tree, mountain, or pebble—was a bubble in that river. Each one shimmered a moment in the light of day, floated along with its comrades, then merged back into the flow. New bubbles appeared, and in turn were absorbed.

It is from this Shinto foundation of universality that Bushido, the Way of the Warrior, arose. Death was not to be feared. A noble death artfully summarized and crowned a man's life. Much more to be feared was a life of deceit and disgrace than death on a true and well-chosen path.

*

Ski Altitude Record

"If I'm going to ski at all," I thought, "I should start from over twenty-six thousand feet." I found the perfect slope in front of my eyes, coming down directly under the southern peak of Mount Everest.

"Let's not miss this opportunity—do it without the oxygen tank." I put on my racing suit, just as if I were going to ski an ordinary slope, and headed toward the south peak.

*

The wind was very strong. A lift on an ordinary ski slope would have shut down in this gale. It was hard enough just to walk. The skis on my shoulder threatened to blow away like a sail. I carried them with both hands through the wind, across the rocky surface of the South Col, making my way toward the snow slope of the southern peak. I expected it to be ice, but it turned out to be good snow. Of course, it was very hard—you could hardly take a step without kicking deep and hard with your boots—but still it could be skied. I climbed up about another thousand feet; above that point, it was blue ice. I put on the skis very carefully, so as not to be blown off by the wind or have the skis slide away.

Genius came up with me, carrying a camera, and asked, "How about some oxygen?" He handed the mask to me with great concern. I couldn't even hear his voice in the whistling wind. I tried a couple of inhalations, but it didn't seem to make any difference, so I decided not to bother and started off.

*

I shot a quick glance at the reddish peak of Makalu. Tibet was drowned in a sea of clouds. The wind pushed me over the border into Tibet. At an elevation of 26,516 feet I took about five big turns and then skied into the South Col, being careful not to slip on the crumbling rocks. Just like children hurrying home after spending too much time playing, we headed for the starting area. I wasn't carrying crampons, but trusted in Genius's technique. I only slipped once on the ice before I reached the spot where Don-chan and Girmi stood. It was already past noon. I could hear Amma's voice in the transceiver saying, "Right now, two people—no, one more—three people have started to come down from the South Col." When I looked up, I could see Ang Pema, carrying a parachute, and Otaki, and Ishiguro coming down toward us.

*

We stand together on a narrow ledge. The tiny platform that we carved with ice axes out of the steep snow slope looks ready to crumble beneath us. We have tied ourselves together with ropes to prevent a fall. If I fall, that would be the end—a three-thousand-foot vertical slide into the Bergschrund. Somehow, through the tangle of safety ropes, I put the parachute harness on. There are about seven belts, but since I've practiced attaching them for months, I do it rather quickly. My gloves are too cumbersome; I hand them to Ang Pema so they will not blow away, and do everything with my bare hands.

To inflate the protective jacket, all I have to do is blow

into the pipe on my chest. Maybe because I'm nervous, I can't complete the transceiver connections. It's cold and my fingers keep getting stuck to the metal; I fumble for two or three minutes. Suddenly it connects.

*

The transceiver crackles in my helmet. When I was in Shangri-La, I could hear broadcasts from Red China; I'm hoping that won't happen here. It seems to be all right. The oxygen pressure is fine. It will last for twenty minutes at this height. I have trouble connecting the mask to the oxygen tank, but the minute I relax, it fits. I wonder which way the wind is going to change in the next few minutes. *My mind is a hummingbird, flitting across the tangle of dreams and necessities.*

*

With all my years of practice, I thought it would be easy to put on the skis, but on this narrow terrace of snow, the skis want to slide off, and when I bend down, my shoulder bumps into the steep wall of the uphill slope. I cannot move, especially after I put the parachute on. Girmi steadies my skis as I insert my boot by sense of touch. The binding snaps in place with a solid, reassuring sound. I hook the rip cord of the parachute onto my right thumb through the strap of my right pole. If this slips while I'm going down, the parachute will not open.

I grab my left ski pole and lower the helmet visor. From the control center, I can hear the reports from Base Camp, Camp 3, Camp 4, and the control center, giving wind speed and direction, but there is no way to really know what the wind is like on the downhill course itself.

*

"All right, fine . . ." I ask Amma at the control center to read out the check list. I thought everything was complete, but I forgot one thing—to strap the helmet under my chin—done. All this preparation took about thirty minutes.

*

The Final Act

Observing the wind, I can see what's left of the jet stream, as it whirls into the south wall. If I'm chased by this wind, it will flatten the parachute. The chute will only open when the wind turns around and blows uphill. Is the parachute really going to open? Has anybody ever tried opening a parachute at twenty-six thousand feet, on skis? I never got around to asking.

*

I know that right from the start the slope is going to be very steep and mean. I know now why Everest climbers avoid this course. It is the shortest route to the South Col, but there is no place to rest on the way. It is a sheet of ice, falling toward an enormous crevasse. Halfway down, at the narrow funnel pinched together by the Geneva Spur and a rocky area that juts out from the south wall, I see a massive concentration of fallen rocks. It looks almost hopeless down there. I have to get through somehow.

*

I can see the control-center tent at the tip of my shoes, like a yellow sesame seed. Cameraman Kanau is supposed to be there with a 1600-mm telephoto lens, but I wonder if he can see me.

In order to head into the wind from the south wall, I move about thirty yards to the left, closer to the Lhotse side. I can see a thin cloud climbing up the slope. As if poised to watch this downhill, Everest floats alone on a sea of clouds that spreads all the way to the Indian Ocean. I decide that my only signal is to start. *Move!*

*

Skis chatter on wind-rippled ice. They bounce and shimmy with increasing violence, but my legs absorb the shock. As I accelerate, I am enveloped in silence. I hear nothing like the roaring winds when I raced in Italy at 107 miles per hour or schussed off the top of Mount Fuji. I am alone in a world without sound. Because the air is so thin and the wind is at my back, I feel nothing, like a rocket streaking through vacuous space.

In about six seconds my speed should reach between 110 and 125 miles per hour. I'll have to pull my rip cord before that. My skis can't possibly edge to a stop on this ice. The chute is my only chance.

*

I yank the rip cord and anxiously wait for the parachute to bloom. Time slows to a groan.

Just as I begin to despair that one more second will bring my speed past all control, I feel the familiar tug.

Usually, when the chute opens, I feel as if I am going to be pulled off the slope, but this time, after the first shock, there is very little resistance. Is it the wind, or the thinness of the air? There is nothing for the chute to hold. It drags along uselessly behind me.

I turn right, toward the south wall, where the chute should grab a little—the speed doesn't seem to change. I turn left, heading for the Geneva Spur. Nothing. I start to drop, hurling through a world without air. I change direction frantically, looking for the wind.

(I heard later that during this time, at control center, Amma reported, "Miura is continuing a very complicated downhill." Hardly! I was desperately trying to establish my braking procedure.)

I switch directions, try a diagonal side slip, and even a straight snowplow, but nothing works. I try to use my edges, but every time, the ice takes control, my skis are caught on a speeding wave of snow which holds me heading straight downhill. I am moving far too fast.

After about thirty seconds or so, I realize all my braking is hopeless, and that I cannot avoid the evil, crevassed jaws of death below. The little bird-beak escape route is impossibly out of reach. "Let's try toward the left side of the Geneva Spur. How about the Lhotse climbing route? What

My chute flapped uselessly behind me. *Photograph copyright © Akira Kotani.*

am I going to do with that menacing ice wall? There must be some way!" My thoughts run completely out of control, but the Watcher within holds cool and solid.

From the exit of the Spur there is only shiny ice, impervious to steel. I can't control my skis' direction. The only chance is to get myself on a snow strip, even if there's a crevasse below it. For some time now, I have begun to think that maybe it is impossible to come out of this alive. My animal instincts howl in terror while my mind keeps looking for a miracle.

*

I recall in a single vivid flash my ancestor Arajiro Miura's *seppuku*. The Taira's forces had triumphed and the surviving princes of Miura fled north in the night with their wives and children.

But Arajiro could not bear flight any better than defeat, so he cut open his belly. It is said that with his dying stroke he severed his own head with such force that it flew through the air and struck a tree, where the teeth bit deep and held. The skull remained there for three years, till a Buddhist priest absolved it of suffering and the lifeless shell rattled to the ground.

As I hurtle toward the Bergschrund I am filled with a desperate vision: with my dying strength I will bite the lips of the jaws of death. Fire with fire, ice against bone, I will bare my fangs and sink them into the edge of the great crevasse. I have descended more than 6000 feet in two minutes.

*

At that very moment my ski catches on something. In the few short seconds before my body hits the ice, I think, "What a time to fall!" Then I feel my spine turn cold. My legs flip from under me and begin scraping the slope. A great sense of resignation comes over me, as though I were drowning in a hopeless sea.

There's nothing I can do. Up to this point, I had been trying to fight with my legs and skis, against the waves of ice, snow, and rock. Now, I have nothing left with which to fight. As my body slides swiftly down the slope, I feel I am being held by a pair of great hands. There is a sense of relief, and I feel I am entering something gigantic with my whole soul.

*

Death

I am falling—falling—there was a place I was supposed to get to. That's where I'm going now. I don't know where it is, but now I can go there. It doesn't feel like dying. It sounds funny to say so, but it's very strange to wait, knowing that you are going, that it's your inescapable destiny. At this moment, I don't know why, but my fleeting curiosity about death is gone.

My mind is unreliable and has already given up, but a spark of me still struggles to escape the closing grip of death. I lift up the strings of the parachute with my right hand and look at the useless, colorful bowl behind me, thinking, "How beautiful." But I am still going as fast as ever.

I wonder how much longer it will take. It seems like such a long time. I'm lost in lonely grays. I wonder what it all meant, being alive? Was it a dream? It doesn't matter now. Dying now, or dying at sixty or eighty is all the same. Even so, I know it is all a dream.

*

Suddenly, there is a rock in front of me. Crash! Time whirls to a stop.

*

I touch the snow lightly, first with my arm, then my head, two or three times into the snow. There is something very warm, nostalgic. A little voice in the corner of my heart says, "Maybe there has been a miracle and I am saved."

Nothing matters in this world without the existence of God; if I return alive, it must be by somebody's will, the will of some great power. Is there something in this world for me to go back to? Should I go back to retrieve the pieces

of myself that God has left behind? Must I search for the rest
of my life?

*

I dwelt in twilight for the next few days. The first flood
of enthusiasm and congratulations from the team members
passed through me unnoticed, like running water when the
glass is full. This shell called Miura had been drained and
swallowed by death. That it was full once again with life
and friendship was too bewildering to believe.

*

> The spirit of the Void is nothing. It is not included in human
> knowledge. By knowing things that exist, you can know that which
> does not exist. That is the Void.
> People think that what they do not understand must be the Void.
> But that is only bewilderment.
> In the Way of strategy those who study to be warriors think that
> whatever they cannot understand in their craft is the Void. That, too,
> is not the true Void.
> With your spirit composed, polish your heart and mind, and
> sharpen perception and sight. When your spirit is utterly clear, and
> the clouds of bewilderment gone, there is the true Void.
> Until you realize the Way, whether by Buddhism, Bushido or
> common sense, you may think the world is incorrect and out of order.
> With forthrightness as the foundation, and your own true spirit as the
> Way, utilize strategy openly and correctly in all matters.
> Then you will view the world as a whole and, taking the Void as
> the Way, you will see the Way as Void.
> Wisdom has existence, principle has existence, the Way has
> existence . . . spirit is an all-embracing empty ring.
>
> MUSASHI "Empty Ring"

*

I Am Alive

We flew toward Katmandu, leaving the peaks of the
Himalayas behind thick clouds. Almost everybody was
dozing, tired from last night—too much *dobon*, and *raksi*
and *chang*, and everybody gambled till morning. In the
airplane were Don-chan, Genius, Zeniya, Kanau, and Otaki.
They were all either snoozing or watching the scenery. I felt
glad to be alive. If I had died, I wouldn't be here to doze
off, or hear the sound of the airplane, or feel we had

accomplished something that will be appreciated by many of our friends.

*

We arrived at Katmandu about an hour later than we had planned. There were heavy clouds, and we detoured in order to avoid bumping into the mountains. The airport looked like a small aircraft carrier. I had finally come back to a world of people. About ten reporters with cameras from the world press greeted us. Among them were the two reporters from Red China, smiling broadly. Somebody put a necklace of Nepal's national flower around my neck. We spent a long hour among the crowd, and then we all lounged under the wing of the airplane to escape the hot sun. Everybody listened to this strange man who had come back alive, talking about skiing Everest. I didn't have a great deal to say.

*

The great climber Wilfrid Noyce once said that danger is a challenge to the masculine ego—a chance to show off. Is that why we carried a 35-mm Cinema-Scope camera, heavy as a small cannon, all the way up there? There was a lot of danger, and we recorded it. We can look back at ourselves and know we were not particularly humble. If there's something possible for a human being to do, even if it involves danger, some of us will try it. Those who do not share this feeling can observe the feat, and approve or disapprove of it, but the fact remains, there will always be those of us who want to make the attempt.

*

Some people may think that an arranged marriage is safer, that finding a partner by oneself is dangerous. Japanese elders generally recommended the arranged marriage, but youth dives into love's ocean on its own and challenges the sharks. Youth must let its blood boil and dare to dream of heroes. Norman Mailer says a hero is a man who argues with the gods, awakes the devils, and competes against them for his vision. Those who have dared to dream always have met opposition.

I wanted to become such a man, at least until the time of Everest. I have begun to change in these last few years since I lived, night and day, with the idea of skiing Everest. Perhaps, having met the world of death, I have learned to respect it.

Anyone can find a peaceful life and happiness on this earth. I didn't have to go to Everest, but still—as if it were my destiny even before I was born—I went ahead, despite the possibility that it might end in death.

*

In "The Dramatic Spirit," the Japanese author Yamazaki says that life is like a morning-glory—a brief but sparkling dream. People who understand this can live bravely and die with confidence, knowing that they remained true to themselves, as did the old Japanese samurai. I made up my mind to live that way. It is a feeling somewhat different from being a hero, or a show-off, or merely courageous. It's a question of spirit—like following an order from a different world or fulfilling an oath, unspoken but binding. I cannot pinpoint the reason for my actions, but I have begun to realize that there is validity in everything one does. It is not on the same plane as being good or bad. Maybe it is love. When, after everything is over, I look back, there is this something which I cannot put into words, something very gentle and sweet. I feel totally alive. I am alive as a person. The things that I wanted to say in this book all boil down to this: in going to Everest, we were trying to repeat the dreams of the samurai—dreams of glory and transient beauty. If life is a dream, let's dream a great dream, until life disappears into eternity, and nothingness.

*

What powerful will brought me back from the world of death at Mount Everest? Whatever it was, I must try to listen to it carefully and follow its directions: as a human being, as a link in the chain of creation, I must be generous to those who are dear to me, and openhearted with the world.

*

In a way our team was like a foreign legion. Although we were told that it was impossible to get such a group of unusual people together, knowing that it was difficult seemed to have helped. We were considerate of each other. We accepted the fact that drunkards were drunkards and gamblers were gamblers; if they wanted to gamble, we let them, and if somebody wanted to be alone, we let him. We all moved as we wished. Still, when someone needed help, we all chipped in, in order to achieve our goal. We all knew that helping each other meant helping ourselves. We did not have to remind ourselves of this; we were professionals.

*

Maybe because we always moved in the shadow of death, we experienced something we could never have found in this modern world. I am glad that this fight was not part of a war or a struggle between people. Maybe that is why all my memories seem a little too sweet, even about death. I have envied and admired people, like Columbus and Lindbergh, who made history with their adventures. I, too, wanted to write a page of history, but that seems a long time ago.

*

In those last days before the great descent, I watched my young colleagues climbing silently, carrying those heavy loads, encouraging the Sherpas without thinking about the danger they themselves were facing; the calm leadership of Don-chan and Amma; the determination of Ishihara's film people, who had never climbed a mountain before; and I thought of those who helped me in Japan and elsewhere. As I stood humbly at the starting point of the downhill, I made up my mind not to let them down. The samurai tradition permeated my thinking, and I knew that death in the face of challenge was worth more to me than a long and easy life of dreams never done.

Miyamoto Musashi, A Brief Biographical Sketch

MIYAMOTO MUSASHI was Japan's greatest swordsman. He was known as *Kensei*, the "saint of swords," for his fierce and uncompromising determination to achieve enlightenment through Bushido, the ethics and skills of battle.

Musashi developed the double-sword fighting technique to its highest art; he was never defeated in combat. By the age of twenty-eight, Musashi had won more than sixty duels, and he quit using steel weapons against single opponents. He roamed Japan, challenging the masters of sword, spear, and staff, and beat them all with a pair of wooden sticks.

Musashi was born in 1584 and orphaned at age seven. He was a large, rough-and-tumble boy, and he slew his first opponent, an armed and able samurai, with a stick at the age of thirteen.

Musashi grew up in a nation at constant war. It was the age of the warlords, desperately fighting for the prize of the shogunate. Death and violence were common currency.

Before he retired to his cave, Musashi fought in six wars and defeated more than a hundred opponents in one-on-one combat.

Musashi followed the Bushido tradition of cultivating the arts of life as well as death, and became a master poet, painter, and sculptor.

In 1643, at the age of fifty-nine, Musashi quit the world for a secluded cave. And there, two years later, a few weeks before his peaceful demise, Musashi wrote *The Way of Five Rings*—the essence of a lifetime on the edge of death and challenge.

*

The selections used in this book from *Go Rin No Sho*, expressing the samurai philosophy of Miyamoto Musashi, are the interpretations of the authors.